Keys to Learning

Skills and Strategies for Newcomers

Anna Uhl Chamot

Catharine W. Keatley

Kristina Anstrom

Longman

Keys to Learning

Skills and Strategies for Newcomers

Pearson Education, 10 Bank Street, White Plains, NY 10606

Vice president, primary and secondary editorial: Ed Lamprich
Publisher: Sherri Pemberton
Vice president, director of production and design: Rhea Banker
Senior production editor: Jane Townsend
Vice president, U.S. marketing: Kate McLoughlin
Senior manufacturing buyer: Edith Pullman
Photo research: Kirchoff/Wohlberg, Inc.
Cover design: Rhea Banker, Tara Mayer Raucci
Text design and composition: Kirchoff/Wohlberg, Inc.
Text font: ITC Franklin Gothic
Text, illustration, and photo credits: See page 264.

Contributors
Charles Green, Ron Ottaviano, Rebecca Rauff, Kevin Sharpe,
and Mairead Stack

Library of Congress Cataloging-in-Publication Data
Chamot, Ana Uhl.
  Keys to learning: skills and strategies for newcomers/Anna Uhl Chamot,
Catharine W. Keatley, Kristina Anstrom.
    p. cm.
  Includes index.
  ISBN 0-13-189221-5
  1. English language—Textbooks for foreign speakers. 2. Study skills—
Problems, exercises, etc. I. Keatley, Catharine W. II. Anstrom, Kristina. III.
Title.
  PE1128.C475 2004
  428.2'4—dc22

                                                    2004002208

LONGMAN ON THE **WEB**

Longman.com offers online resources for
teachers and students. Access our Companion
Websites, our online catalog, and our local
offices around the world.

Visit us at **longman.com**.

ISBN: 0-13-189221-5

Printed in the United States of America
1 2 3 4 5 6 7 8 9 10–RRD–08 07 06 05 04

About the Authors

Anna Uhl Chamot is professor of secondary education and faculty adviser for ESL in the Department of Teacher Preparation and Special Education at The George Washington University. She is a researcher and teacher educator in content-based second-language learning and language-learning strategies. She co-designed and has written extensively about the Cognitive Academic Language Learning Approach (CALLA) and implemented the CALLA model in the Arlington public schools in Virginia. She received her Ph.D. in applied linguistics from the University of Texas at Austin. She is co-author of the Shining Star program.

Catharine W. Keatley is associate director of the National Capital Language Resource Center for The George Washington University, Georgetown University, and The Center for Applied Linguistics. She taught English as a foreign language with the Peace Corps in Senegal and received her M.A. from New York University in remedial reading and learning disabilities. After traveling and living in a number of different countries, she received her Ph.D. from the University of Hong Kong, where she studied cognitive psychology with a focus on bilingual memory.

Kristina Anstrom is the assistant director of the Center for Equity and Excellence in Education at The George Washington University. She has been involved in the education of English language learners as a teacher, researcher, and teacher educator. She has worked with teachers and teacher educators at the K–12 and university levels to help them design more inclusive curricula and learning environments for English language learners. She received her doctorate in education from The George Washington University.

CONTENTS

SCOPE AND SEQUENCE vi

INTRODUCTION: GETTING STARTED 2

- Introductions 4
- Classroom Objects 5
- Classroom Commands 6
- Days of the Week 7
- The Alphabet 8
- Numbers 1–20 9
- Numbers 20–100 10
- Time 11
- Months of the Year 12
- Dates 13

CHARACTERS 14

UNIT 1: NEW FRIENDS 16

- Chapter 1   What's your name? 18
- Chapter 2   What classes do you have? 28
- Chapter 3   This is a calculator. 38

UNIT 2: AT SCHOOL 48

- Chapter 4   Where's the gym? 50
- Chapter 5   What's your address? 60
- Chapter 6   You were late yesterday. 70

UNIT 3: AT HOME 80

- Chapter 7   What are you doing? 82
- Chapter 8   I have to work. 92
- Chapter 9   You came to our party! 102

UNIT 4: AROUND TOWN 112

- Chapter 10 How much is it? 114
- Chapter 11 She needs some lettuce. 124
- Chapter 12 He's the cutest guy at school. 134

UNIT 5: Friends & Family 144

- Chapter 13 He's going to fall! 146
- Chapter 14 Hey! The lights went out! 156
- Chapter 15 We'll have a study group. 166

UNIT 6: Feelings & Hobbies 176

- Chapter 16 I sometimes study with my friends. 178
- Chapter 17 You should get some rest. 188
- Chapter 18 It was too easy. 198

Additional Resources 208

Focus on Content

- Life Science How Nature Works:
  Ecosystems and Food Chains 210
- Physical Science The Universe:
  Earth and the Milky Way 212
- Math Solving Word Problems:
  Mathematics in Everyday Life 214
- Literature Poetry:
  Understanding Images 216
- Social Studies The United States:
  Reading Maps of Our Country 218
- History Martin Luther King Jr.:
  An American Hero 220

Vocabulary Handbook 222

Grammar Handbook 234

Word Analysis 250

The Writing Process 252

Using a Dictionary 256

Learning Strategies 258

Glossary 259

Topical Index 261

Scope and Sequence

	Grammar	Phonics	Learning Strategies	Writing
Unit 1 New Friends				
Chapter 1 What's your name?	Pronouns; Present tense of *be*: statements; *yes/no* questions	The alphabet; Consonants and vowels; Alphabetical order	Preview	Write a paragraph about yourself
Chapter 2 What classes do you have?	Present tense of *have*: statements, *yes/no* questions; Plural nouns; Possessive adjectives	Short vowel sounds: /a/ as in *cat*, /i/ as in *sit*, and /o/ as in *hot*	Sound out; Preview	Write a paragraph about your favorite class
Chapter 3 This is a calculator.	Articles: *a* and *an;* Demonstrative pronouns: *this, that, these,* and *those;* Possessive of singular and plural nouns	Short vowel sounds: /e/ as in *bed* and /u/ as in *cup*	Sound out; Preview	Write a paragraph about things in your backpack
Unit 2 At School				
Chapter 4 Where's the gym?	Prepositions of location: *in, on, under,* and *next to; Where* questions with *be; There is* and *there are*	Consonant sounds: /ch/ as in *lunch* and /sh/ as in *English*	Sound out; Make predictions	Write a paragraph about places in your school
Chapter 5 What's your address?	*What* questions with *be;* Present tense of regular verbs: statements; *yes/no* questions; Statements with *can; Yes/no* questions with *can*	Consonant blends at the beginning of a word, such as *class, pretty,* and *student*	Sound out; Use selective attention	Fill out a form with your personal information
Chapter 6 You were late yesterday.	*What* questions with *do; What* + noun; Past tense of *be*: statements; *yes/no* questions	Consonant blends at the end of a word, such as *find, went,* and *best*	Sound out; Make predictions	Write a paragraph about your day

	Grammar	Phonics	Learning Strategies	Writing
Unit 3 At Home				
Chapter 7 What are you doing?	Present continuous tense: statements; *what* questions; *yes/no* questions; Object pronouns	Long vowel sounds: /ā/ as in *came*, /ī/ as in *like*, /ō/ as in *close*, and /yōo/ as in *use*	Sound out; Make predictions	Write a dialogue about what you are doing
Chapter 8 I have to work.	Simple present tense and present continuous tense; Statements with *like, have,* and *want* + infinitive; *What* questions with *like, have,* and *want* + infinitive; *Yes/no* questions with *like, have,* and *want* + infinitive	Long vowel sound: /ā/ as in *take, wait,* and *say*	Sound out; Use what you know	Write a paragraph about a classmate
Chapter 9 You came to our party!	Past tense of regular and irregular verbs: statements; *yes/no* questions	Long vowel sound: /ē/ as in *me, read, meet, happy,* and *piece*	Sound out; Make inferences	Write a letter to a friend
Unit 4 Around Town				
Chapter 10 How much is it?	Information questions with *be*: present tense; past tense; Information questions with *do*: present tense; past tense; Questions with *how much*	Long vowel sound: /ī/ as in *hi, my, time, pie,* and *right*	Sound out; Make predictions	Write a script for a fashion show
Chapter 11 She needs some lettuce.	Count and non-count nouns; *Some* and *any*; Conjunctions: *and, but,* and *so*	Long vowel sound: /ō/ as in *go, Joe, those, coat,* and *know*	Sound out; Use selective attention	Write a paragraph about your favorite food
Chapter 12 He's the cutest guy at school.	Comparative adjectives; Superlative adjectives; Comparatives and superlatives with *more* and *most*	Long vowel sound: /yōo/ as in *use, unit,* and *few*	Sound out; Use what you know	Write words for a song

	Grammar	Phonics	Learning Strategies	Writing
Unit 5 Friends & Family				
Chapter 13 He's going to fall!	Future tense with *be going to*: statements; *yes/no* questions; information questions; Commands	Other vowel sound: /o͞o/ as in *school*, *rule*, *true*, and *new*	Sound out; Make inferences	Write a dialogue about your weekend plans
Chapter 14 Hey! The lights went out!	Past continuous tense: statements; *yes/no* questions; information questions; Possessive pronouns; Questions with *whose*	Other vowel sound: /o͝o/ as in *look*	Sound out; Use selective attention	Write a paragraph about something that happened to you
Chapter 15 We'll have a study group.	Future tense with *will*: statements; *yes/no* questions; information questions; Statements with *may* and *might*	Other vowel sound: /ô/ as in *auditorium* and *saw*	Sound out; Personalize	Write a few paragraphs about one of your goals
Unit 6 Feelings & Hobbies				
Chapter 16 I sometimes study with my friends.	Adverbs of frequency; Adverbs of frequency with *be*; *How often* and expressions of frequency; Gerunds as objects of verbs	Other vowel sound: /oi/ as in *voice* and *enjoy*	Sound out; Use what you know	Write a paragraph about a classmate's hobby or interest
Chapter 17 You should get some rest.	Statements with *should*; *Yes/no* questions with *should*; Statements with *could*; *Because* clauses	Other vowel sound: /ou/ as in *out* and *now*	Sound out; Use selective attention	Write a letter giving advice to someone
Chapter 18 It was too easy.	Comparatives and superlatives: irregular adjectives; *Too* and *not enough*; Statements with *used to*; *Yes/no* questions with *used to*	Other vowel sound: /ûr/ as in *hurt*, *first*, and *her*	Sound out; Make predictions	Write a story about a character

To the Student

Welcome to

Keys to Learning

This program will help you learn how to listen, speak, read, and write in English. You will learn about English grammar. You will also learn new words and expressions that you can use in everyday conversation.

Each chapter has a story about a group of teenagers and the things that happen to them at home, at school, and around town. You will read about them while you learn English.

Each chapter also gives you tips, or learning strategies, that will help you to learn. You can use these strategies in every one of your classes.

Before you begin each chapter, look at the pictures. They will help you understand what you are reading. Also, ask questions about what you are reading. This will help you learn even more.

The Learning Log at the end of each chapter will help you review and understand how you learn. Your English will get better as you learn and practice.

We hope you enjoy *Keys to Learning*!

Anna Uhl Chamot
Catharine W. Keatley
Kristina Anstrom

GETTING STARTED

GOALS

In Getting Started you will learn about . . .

- introductions
- classroom objects
- classroom commands
- days of the week
- the alphabet
- numbers 1–100
- time
- months of the year
- dates (ordinal numbers 1st–31st)

Introductions

A. Look at the name. Then write your first and last name in your notebook.

Isabel   Estrada
▲ first name   ▲ last name (family name)

B. Listen and say the dialogue.

A: Hello.

B: Hi. What's your name?

A: My name is Isabel Estrada.

B: I'm Chan Lee. Nice to meet you.

A: Nice to meet you, too.

C. Practice the dialogue with a classmate. Take turns reading each part. Then practice again. Use your own names.

D. Look at the picture. Listen and say the names in the picture. Then take turns practicing the dialogue with a classmate using the names in the picture.

Ms. Smith   Edgar Lopez   Juni Kato   Anna Arias   Mr. Dean

E. Close your book and stand up. Use the dialogue to meet as many classmates as possible.

Classroom Objects

A. Listen and say the names of the classroom objects.

1. a chalkboard
9. a bookcase
2. a book
3. a notebook
8. a chair
4. a pen
7. a table
6. an eraser
5. a pencil

B. Write the names of the objects in your notebook.

C. Listen and say the dialogue.

A: What's this?

B: It's a book.

D. Practice the dialogue with a classmate. Take turns reading each part. Then practice again. Use the names of different objects.

Classroom Commands

A. **A.** Listen and say the classroom commands.

1. Stand up.

2. Get in pairs.

3. Sit down.

4. Raise your hand.

5. Open your notebook.

6. Get your pencil.

7. Write your name.

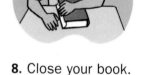

8. Close your book.

B. Listen to your teacher and follow his or her commands.

C. Listen and say the dialogue.

A: Open your book.

B: Okay, Ms. Estrada.

D. Practice the dialogue with a classmate. Take turns reading each part. Then practice again. Give different commands. Use your own last names with "Mr." or "Ms."

Days of the Week

A. Listen and say the days of the week.

Sunday Monday Tuesday Wednesday Thursday Friday Saturday

B. Listen and say the dialogue.

A: What day is it?

B: It's Monday.

C. Practice the dialogue with a classmate. Take turns reading each part. Then practice again. Use different days of the week.

D. Write the days of the week in order in your notebook.

E. Play this game with a classmate. Say, "Today is Monday. Tomorrow is . . ." Your classmate must complete the sentence: "Tuesday." Take turns. Use different days of the week. Work quickly. If your classmate says the wrong day, you get 1 point. The person with the most points wins.

The Alphabet

A. Listen and say the letters of the alphabet.

Aa Bb Cc Dd Ee Ff Gg Hh Ii Jj Kk Ll Mm

Nn Oo Pp Qq Rr Ss Tt Uu Vv Ww Xx Yy Zz

B. Listen to the ABC song.

C. Listen and say the dialogue.

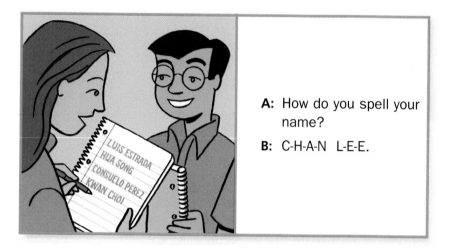

A: How do you spell your name?

B: C-H-A-N L-E-E.

D. Practice the dialogue with a classmate. Take turns reading each part. Then practice again. Spell your own names.

E. Stand up and talk to different classmates. Ask and answer how to spell your names. Write the names in your notebook.

Numbers 1–20

A. Listen and say the numbers.

1 one	**6** six	**11** eleven	**16** sixteen
2 two	**7** seven	**12** twelve	**17** seventeen
3 three	**8** eight	**13** thirteen	**18** eighteen
4 four	**9** nine	**14** fourteen	**19** nineteen
5 five	**10** ten	**15** fifteen	**20** twenty

B. Write the numbers 1–20 in your notebook. Then write the number word next to each number.

C. Listen and say the dialogue.

A: How old are you?

B: I'm fifteen.

D. Practice the dialogue with a classmate. Take turns reading each part. Then practice again. Use your own ages.

E. Close your books and stand up. Use the dialogue to find out the ages of as many classmates as possible.

Numbers 20–100

🎧 **A.** Listen and say the numbers.

20 twenty	**24** twenty-four	**28** twenty-eight	**50** fifty	**80** eighty
21 twenty-one	**25** twenty-five	**29** twenty-nine	**60** sixty	**90** ninety
22 twenty-two	**26** twenty-six	**30** thirty	**70** seventy	**100** one hundred
23 twenty-three	**27** twenty-seven	**40** forty		

B. Write the number words for these numbers in your notebook.
The numbers 30–99 follow the same pattern as 20–29.

1. **31** *thirty-one*
2. **42**
3. **53**
4. **64**

5. **75**
6. **86**
7. **97**
8. **28**

9. **49**
10. **66**
11. **37**
12. **82**

🎧 **C.** Listen and say the dialogue.

A: What's twenty-three plus thirty-one?

B: It's fifty-four.

D. Practice the dialogue with a classmate. Take turns reading each part. Then practice again. Use different numbers.

Time

 A. Listen and say the times.

1. one o'clock

2. one oh five

3. one ten

4. one fifteen

5. one twenty

6. one twenty-five

7. one thirty

8. one thirty-five

9. one forty

10. one forty-five

11. one fifty

12. one fifty-five

B. Write the words for these times in your notebook.

1. 7:15	*seven fifteen*	**5.**	8:00	**9.**	1:55		
2. 9:35		**6.**	6:05	**10.**	12:33		
3. 3:20		**7.**	11:25	**11.**	4:48		
4. 5:45		**8.**	2:10	**12.**	10:02		

 C. Listen and say the dialogue.

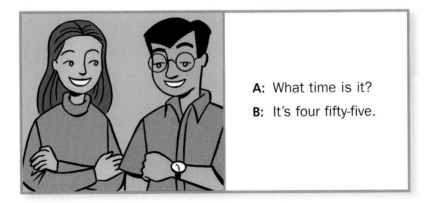

A: What time is it?

B: It's four fifty-five.

D. Practice the dialogue with a classmate. Take turns reading each part. Then practice again. Use different times.

Months of the Year

A. Listen and say the months.

1. January

2. February

3. March

4. April

5. May

6. June

7. July

8. August

9. September

10. October

11. November

12. December

B. Listen and say the dialogue.

A: What month is it?

B: It's April.

C. Practice the dialogue with a classmate. Take turns reading each part.
Then practice again. Use different months of the year.

Dates

A. Listen and say the ordinal numbers.

1st first	**8th** eighth	**15th** fifteenth	**22nd** twenty-second	**29th** twenty-ninth
2nd second	**9th** ninth	**16th** sixteenth	**23rd** twenty-third	**30th** thirtieth
3rd third	**10th** tenth	**17th** seventeenth	**24th** twenty-fourth	**31st** thirty-first
4th fourth	**11th** eleventh	**18th** eighteenth	**25th** twenty-fifth	
5th fifth	**12th** twelfth	**19th** nineteenth	**26th** twenty-sixth	
6th sixth	**13th** thirteenth	**20th** twentieth	**27th** twenty-seventh	
7th seventh	**14th** fourteenth	**21st** twenty-first	**28th** twenty-eighth	

B. Listen and say the dialogue.

A: What's the date?

B: It's September fifteenth.

C. Practice the dialogue with a classmate. Take turns reading each part. Then practice again. Use different dates.

D. Spell out the birthdays of these famous people in your notebook.

1. Mandy Moore
4/10
April tenth

2. Tiger Woods
12/30

3. Jackie Chan
4/7

4. Ashley Olsen
6/13

Carmen

Carlos

Sophie

Mei

Samir

Maria

Liliana

Bic

Pablo

UNIT 1

NEW FRIENDS

GOALS

In Unit 1 you will learn to . . .

- listen to and read dialogues and stories about students at school

- ask and answer questions about names, countries, languages, and class schedules

- identify the letters of the alphabet and the names of vowels and consonants

- put words in alphabetical order

- use numbers from 1 to 10

- write about yourself, your favorite class, and the things in your backpack

- use the learning strategy *Sound Out*

Chapter 1

What's your name?

GETTING READY

Look at the picture. What things can you name in English? Say the words.

LISTENING AND READING

A. Listen to the dialogue. Then answer this question: What is the teacher's name?

B. Read the dialogue.

Good Morning

Mr. Gomez: Good morning, students. I'm your English teacher. My name is Mr. Gomez. I'm from the United States. I speak English and Spanish.

* * * * *

Mr. Gomez: Hello. What's your name?

Bic: My name is Bic.

Mr. Gomez: Nice to meet you, Bic.

Bic: Nice to meet you, too, Mr. . . . umm . . .

Mr. Gomez: Mr. Gomez. G-O-M-E-Z. Gomez.

Bic: Mr. Gomez. Thank you. Umm . . . nice to meet you!

* * * * *

Mr. Gomez: Hi! What's your name?

Carmen: My name is Carmen Alvarez.

Mr. Gomez: And what's your name?

Carlos: My name is Carlos Alvarez.

Mr. Gomez: Is Carmen your sister?

Carlos: Yes, she is.

Carmen: Yes, he's my brother and I'm his sister. We're from Mexico.

* * * * *

Mr. Gomez: What's your name?

Maria: My . . . my . . . my name . . . is . . . is . . . umm . . .

| Mr. Gomez: | Are you okay? |
| Maria: | Yes, I . . . am. I . . . umm . . . am . . . nervous. |

★ ★ ★ ★ ★

Carmen:	Wow! She's *very* nervous. What's her name?
Carlos:	She's very *pretty*! What *is* her name?
Carmen:	Carlos!

 Pair and Group Work

A. Read the dialogue with a classmate.

B. Act out the dialogue in groups of five.

VOCABULARY

Words		Expressions
student	brother	Good morning.
English	Mexico	Nice to meet you.
teacher	okay	Nice to meet you, too.
the United States	nervous	Thank you.
Spanish	very	Hello. / Hi.
sister	pretty	Wow!

A. Read and say the vocabulary. Then write the vocabulary in your notebook.

B. Use word analysis to study the vocabulary (see page 250, Step 1).

C. Find the vocabulary in the dialogue. Then read the sentences that use the vocabulary.

D. Choose two words from the word box. In your notebook, write two sentences using these words.

Grammar 1

Pronouns

▲ I   ▲ you   ▲ she   ▲ he

▲ it   ▲ we   ▲ you   ▲ they

A. Write the numbers 1–5 in your notebook. Match each item in the left-hand column with a pronoun from the right-hand column. Write the letter of the correct answer in your notebook.

1. ___*c*___ Mr. Gomez and I   **a.** you
2. _____ Carmen and Maria   **b.** she
3. _____ Pablo and you   **c.** we
4. _____ Carmen   **d.** they
5. _____ Carlos   **e.** he

B. Copy the sentences into your notebook. Then fill in the blanks with the correct pronouns.

1. <u>Carmen</u> is from Mexico.   ___*She*___ is from Mexico.
2. <u>Carlos and Carmen</u> are from Mexico.   _____ are from Mexico.
3. <u>The book</u> is from the United States.   _____ is from the United States.
4. <u>Maria and I</u> are from El Salvador.   _____ are from El Salvador.
5. <u>Mr. Gomez</u> is from the United States.   _____ is from the United States.

Grammar 2

Present Tense of *be*: Statements

Affirmative Statements				Negative Statements				
I	am			I	am			
You	are			You	are			
He/She It	is	from Mexico.		He/She It	is		not	from Mexico.
We You They	are			We You They	are			

Contractions			
I am	= I'm	we are	= we're
you are	= you're	you are	= you're
he is	= he's	they are	= they're
she is	= she's		
it is	= it's		

A. Copy the sentences into your notebook. Then fill in the blanks with the correct pronoun and the correct form of *be*. Use contractions.

1. *They're* not students. (They)
2. _____ from the United States. (I)
3. _____ nervous. (It)
4. _____ not from Mexico. (He)
5. _____ teachers. (We)

B. Change each statement from affirmative to negative or from negative to affirmative. Write the new sentences in your notebook.

1. He's a teacher. *He's not a teacher.*
2. I'm not from Peru. *I'm from Peru.*
3. You're a student.
4. She's my sister.
5. It's not pretty.

Word Study

The Alphabet

A. Review the alphabet. Say the names of the letters.

B. Write the alphabet in capital letters in your notebook. Next, write the alphabet in small letters.

Consonants and Vowels

A. As a class, review the names of the consonants and their sounds.

b c d f g h j k l m n p q r s t v w x y z

B. As a class, review the names of the vowels.

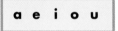

C. Write your name in your notebook. Begin it with a capital letter. Does your name begin with a consonant or a vowel?

Alphabetical Order

Use the alphabet to help you write words in alphabetical order.

A. Write the numbers 1–8 in your notebook. Then write the names below in alphabetical order.

Carmen	Maria	Samir	Mei
Liliana	Pablo	Carlos	Bic

EXAMPLE: **1.** *Bic* **2.** *Carlos* **3.** *Carmen*

B. Write the names of your classmates in your notebook. Then work with a classmate to write the names in alphabetical order.

Grammar 3

Present tense of *be*: Yes/No Questions

Am	I			you	are.		you're	
Are	you			I	am.		I'm	
Is	he/she it	from Mexico?	Yes,	he/she it	is.	No,	he's she's it's	not.
Are	we you they			you we they	are.		you're we're they're	

A. Copy the questions into your notebook. Then write the answers.

1. Is Carlos from El Salvador? *No, he's not.*
2. Is Mr. Gomez from the United States?
3. Are Carlos and Carmen from Mexico?
4. Is Carmen from the United States?
5. Are you from Mexico?

B. Read the conversation. Then listen.

A: Are you from Peru?

B: No, I'm not. I'm from Mexico.

C. Practice the conversation in Exercise B with a classmate. Then make new conversations using your own information.

Reading

Preview the reading. Look at the picture of Maria. How does she feel? How do you feel in a new school? Talk about it with a classmate.

A New School

This is Maria Lopez. She is from El Salvador. She is a new student at Washington School. Maria speaks Spanish. Her teacher is Mr. Gomez. He speaks Spanish and English.

Mr. Gomez speaks to Bic, Carmen, and her brother Carlos. Carmen and Carlos are from Mexico.

Maria is very nervous. She is in a new school. She says, "My . . . my . . . my name is . . . is . . . umm . . ."

Carmen says, "Wow! She's *very* nervous. What's her name?"

Carlos says, "She's very *pretty*! What *is* her name?"

AFTER YOU READ

A. Work in groups of three to act out the story. Look at the story again. Read the words in quotation marks to act out the story about Maria, Carmen, and Carlos.

B. True or false? In your notebook, write *True* or *False* for each statement.

1. Maria is a student at Washington School. *True.*
2. Carmen is a teacher.
3. Carlos is not from Mexico.
4. Mr. Gomez is a teacher.
5. Maria is very nervous.

Check your work. How many of your answers are correct? Write the number of correct answers in your notebook.

Keep Trying!   Great Work!

Writing

BEFORE YOU WRITE

A. You are going to write a paragraph about yourself. First, read the paragraph below.

> *My name is Pablo Cortez. I am a student at Washington School. I am from Colombia. I speak Spanish and English.*

B. Read the *Before I Write* checklist. In your notebook, write your name, your school, your country, and your language.

WRITE THIS!

Read the *While I Write* checklist. In your notebook, write a paragraph about yourself. Ask your teacher for new words.

AFTER YOU WRITE

A. Read the *After I Write* checklist. Then check your work.

B. Read your paragraph to a classmate. Then listen to your classmate read his or her paragraph.

C. Write a final copy of your paragraph in your notebook.

Before I Write

▶ Study the model.

▶ Think about myself.

▶ Make notes about . . .

  my name
  the name of my school
  the name of my country
  my language (or languages)

While I Write

▶ Put a **capital letter** at the beginning of a sentence.

  My name is Pablo Cortez.

▶ Put a **capital letter** at the beginning of a name of a person, place, country, or language.

  Pablo Cortez
  Washington School
  Colombia
  Spanish

▶ Put a **period** at the end of a sentence.

  I speak Spanish and English.

After I Write

▶ Did I put a capital letter at the beginning of a sentence?

▶ Did I put a capital letter at the beginning of a name of a person, place, country, or language?

▶ Did I put a period at the end of a sentence?

Learning Log

◆ VOCABULARY

Read the words and expressions. Then copy them into your notebook.
Underline the words and expressions you need to review.

Nouns				Expressions
Countries	***Languages***	***People***	***Other***	Good morning.
El Salvador	English	brother	school	Hello. / Hi.
Mexico	Spanish	sister		Nice to meet you.
the United States		student		Nice to meet you, too.
		teacher		Thank you.
				Wow!
Verbs	**Adjectives**	**Adverb**	**Question Word**	
be (am, is, are)	nervous	very	what	
say	new			
speak	okay			
	pretty			

◆ LANGUAGE

Copy the checklist into your notebook. Check what you know. Review what you
need to know.

I can . . .

_____ read and understand the dialogue "Good Morning"

_____ use pronouns correctly

_____ ask and answer questions using the present tense of *be*

_____ say the names of the letters of the alphabet

_____ put words in alphabetical order

_____ read and understand the story "A New School"

_____ write a paragraph about myself

◆ SELF-EVALUATION QUESTIONS

Answer the questions in your notebook.

1. What is easy in Chapter 1? What is difficult in Chapter 1?
2. How can you learn the things that are difficult?

Chapter 2

What classes do you have?

GETTING READY

Look at the picture. What things can you name in English? Say the words.

LISTENING AND READING

A. Listen to the dialogue. Then answer this question: What is Carmen's favorite class?

B. Read the dialogue.

Our Schedules

Liliana: Hey, Carmen. What's your schedule?

Carmen: Well, I have lunch now. Then I have P.E. . . . .

Liliana: Oh. My schedule is different. I have P.E. now, then I have lunch. After lunch I have math.

Carmen: Good! We have math together! Math is my favorite class.

Liliana: It's my favorite class, too. After math do you have science?

Carmen: Yes, I do. We have Mrs. Kim, right?

Liliana: That's right. Then I have music.

Carmen: Me, too! Our schedules are almost the same!

Liliana: Yes, they are.

Carmen:	Hey! It's Maria. Hi, Maria. How are you?
Maria:	I'm fine. And you?
Carmen:	Fine, thanks.
Liliana:	What's your schedule, Maria?
Maria:	I have . . . I have . . .
Liliana:	Maria, you have music, lunch, math, science, and P.E. Our schedules are almost the same!
Maria:	That's great!

Pair and Group Work

A. Read the dialogue with a classmate.

B. Act out the dialogue in groups of three.

VOCABULARY

Words		Expressions
schedule	together	Hey!
lunch	favorite	Good!
now	class	That's right.
P.E.	science	How are you?
different	music	I'm fine. And you?
after	almost	Fine, thanks.
math	same	That's great!

A. Read and say the vocabulary. Then write the vocabulary in your notebook.

B. Use word analysis to study the vocabulary (see page 250, Step 1).

C. Find the vocabulary in the dialogue. Then read the sentences that use the vocabulary.

D. Choose three words from the word box. In your notebook, write three sentences using these words.

Grammar 1

Present Tense of *have*: Affirmative Statements

I You	**have**	
He/She	**has**	lunch now.
We You They	**have**	

A. Copy the sentences below into your notebook. Then look at the schedules. Write *True* or *False*.

Schedule **Carmen Alvarez**	
Period 1:	art
Period 2:	history
Period 3:	English
Period 4:	lunch
Period 5:	P.E.
Period 6:	math
Period 7:	science
Period 8:	music

Schedule **Carlos Alvarez**	
Period 1:	art
Period 2:	history
Period 3:	English
Period 4:	lunch
Period 5:	music
Period 6:	P.E.
Period 7:	science
Period 8:	math

1. Carlos and Carmen have the same English class.   *True.*
2. Carlos has music after lunch.
3. Carmen and Carlos have math together.
4. Carlos has art. Then he has history.
5. Carmen and Carlos have the same P.E. class.

B. Copy the sentences into your notebook. Then fill in the blanks with the correct form of *have*.

1. You ___*have*___ art now.
2. I _____ music after lunch.
3. We _____ history together.
4. They _____ English with Mr. Gomez.
5. He _____ science with Mrs. Kim.

Grammar 2

Present Tense of *have*: Negative Statements

I You	do not have	
He/She	does not have	lunch now.
We You They	do not have	

do not	= don't
does not	= doesn't

Change each statement from affirmative to negative. Write the new sentences in your notebook. Use contractions.

1. Liliana has P.E. now. *Liliana doesn't have P.E. now.*
2. Carmen has math with Liliana.
3. Maria and Liliana have English class together.
4. I have math after lunch.
5. You have seven classes.

Present Tense of *have*: Yes/No Questions

Do	I you			Yes,	you I	do.	No,	you I	don't.
Does	he/she	have	math after lunch?		he/she	does.		he/she	doesn't.
Do	we you they				you we they	do.		you we they	don't.

Look at the sentences in the previous exercise. Change each statement to a question. Write the questions in your notebook.

EXAMPLE: *Does Liliana have P.E. now?*

Word Study

Short Vowel Sounds: /a/, /i/, /o/

The letter *a* can stand for the short vowel sound /a/ as in *cat*.
The letter *i* can stand for the short vowel sound /i/ as in *sit*.
The letter *o* can stand for the short vowel sound /o/ as in *hot*.

A. Use the learning strategy *Sound Out* and the pictures to read the words.

1. mat

2. cap

3. hat

4. map

5. hit

6. big

7. pig

8. hot

B. Read the sentences aloud. Then copy them into your notebook. Circle the letters that stand for the short vowel sounds /a/, /i/, and /o/.

1. Maria has a pretty hat.
2. Samir has my cap.
3. It is a very big pig.
4. Is the map in your book?
5. My lunch is hot.
6. Hit the ball with your bat.

C. Look at the dialogue on pages 28–29. Find two words with the short vowel sound /a/ and two words with the short vowel sound /i/. Write the words in your notebook.

Grammar 3

Plural Nouns

To make most nouns **plural**, add **-s**.

Singular		Plural
student	⟶	students
book	⟶	books
cap	⟶	caps
pencil	⟶	pencils

If a noun ends in **s**, **x**, **sh**, or **ch**, add **-es** to make it **plural**.

Singular		Plural
class	⟶	classes
box	⟶	boxes
brush	⟶	brushes
lunch	⟶	lunches

Copy the words into your notebook. Then write the plural form of each noun.

1. brother _brothers_   3. desk _____   5. box _____

2. class _____   4. pencil _____   6. schedule _____

Possessive Adjectives

Subject Pronoun	Possessive Adjective	
I	my	**My** name is Mei.
you	your	**Your** name is Carlos.
he	his	**His** name is Mr. Gomez.
she	her	**Her** name is Maria.
it	its	**Its** name is Snowy.
we	our	**Our** names are Carlos and Carmen.
they	their	**Their** names are Samir and Bic.

Copy the sentences into your notebook. Then fill in the blanks with the correct possessive adjective.

Hi! (**1**) _My_ name is Marcos. I'm from Brazil. This is (**2**) _____ sister. (**3**) _____ name is Clara. She's pretty! And this is (**4**) _____ brother. (**5**) _____ name is Luis. My mother and father are here, too. (**6**) _____ names are Ricardo and Helena.

BEFORE YOU READ

Preview the reading. Look at the picture. What class is this?
How do you know? Talk about it with a classmate.

READ THIS!

The Math Class

Mrs. Garcia is the math teacher. Four of her students are boys. Five of her students are girls. Maria, Carmen, and Liliana are in her math class. Carmen and Liliana are very good at math. Carmen loves math.

Carmen's brother, Carlos, does not have math with Carmen and Liliana. He has a different schedule. Carlos does not love math. He is not very good at it. He likes history.

Mrs. Garcia is from Puerto Rico. She speaks two languages. She speaks Spanish and English. The students speak different languages. Five students speak Spanish. One student, Mei, speaks Chinese. She is from China. One student, Samir, speaks Arabic. He is from Lebanon.

The students have math every day. They also have art, English, history, music, science, and P.E.

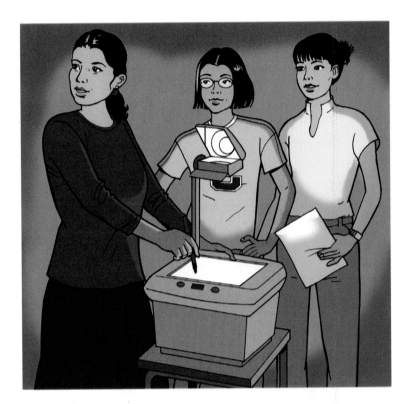

AFTER YOU READ

A. Solve the math problem. Then write the answer in your notebook.

There are _____ students in the math class.

B. True or false? In your notebook, write *True* or *False* for each statement.

1. Carmen and Liliana are good at math.
2. Carlos and Carmen have math together.
3. Eight students speak Spanish.
4. One student speaks Chinese.
5. The students have math every day.

Check your work. How many of your answers are correct? Write the number of correct answers in your notebook.

Keep Trying!　Great Work!

Writing

BEFORE YOU WRITE

A. You are going to write a paragraph about your favorite class. First, read the paragraph below.

> *I have eight classes. My favorite class is math. Mrs. Garcia is my math teacher. She speaks English and Spanish. Five girls and four boys are in my math class. I love math.*

B. Read the *Befor rite* checklist. In your notebook, write your favorite class, the name of the teacher, and the number of girls and boys in the class.

WRITE THIS!

Read the *While I Write* checklist. In your notebook, write a paragraph about your favorite class. Ask your teacher for new words.

AFTER YOU WRITE

A. Read the *After I Write* checklist. Then check your work.

B. Read your paragraph to a classmate. Then listen to your classmate read his or her paragraph.

C. Write a final copy of your paragraph in your notebook.

Before I Write

▶ Study the model.

▶ Think about my classes.

▶ Make notes about . . .

  my favorite class
  the teacher of my favorite class
  the number of girls in that class
  the number of boys in that class

While I Write

▶ **Indent**, or move in, the first line of a paragraph.

  I have eight classes. My favorite class is math.

▶ Put a **capital letter** at the beginning of the name of a language.

  She speaks English and Spanish.

▶ Add an **-s** or **-es** to the end of a word to make it plural.

  Five girls and four boys are in my math class.

After I Write

▶ Did I indent the first line of my paragraph?

▶ Did I put a capital letter at the beginning of the name of a language?

▶ Did I add an -s or -es to the end of a word to make it plural?

Learning Log

◆ VOCABULARY

Read the words and expressions. Then copy them into your notebook.
Underline the words and expressions you need to review.

Nouns					Expressions
Countries	*Languages*	*School Subjects*		*Other*	Fine, thanks.
China	Arabic	art	music	boy	language	Good!
Lebanon	Chinese	English	P.E.	class	lunch	good at . . .
Puerto Rico		history	science	day	schedule	Hey!
		math				How are you?

Verb	Adjectives		Adverbs		Question Word	I'm fine. And you?
have	different	great	after	now	how	not very good at . . .
	every	same	almost	then		That's great!
	favorite		also	together		That's right.

◆ LANGUAGE and LEARNING STRATEGIES

Copy the checklist into your notebook. Check what you know. Review what you
need to know.

I can . . .

_____ read and understand the dialogue "Our Schedules"

_____ ask and answer questions using the present tense of *have*

_____ spell the plural form of nouns correctly

_____ read and use new words with the short vowel sounds /a/, /i/, and /o/

_____ use the learning strategy *Sound Out* to read new words

_____ read and understand the story "The Math Class"

_____ write a paragraph about my favorite class

◆ SELF-EVALUATION QUESTIONS

Answer the questions in your notebook.

1. What is easy in Chapter 2? What is difficult in Chapter 2?
2. How can you learn the things that are difficult?

Chapter 3

This is a calculator.

GETTING READY

Look at the picture. What things can you name in English? Say the words.

LISTENING AND READING

A. Listen to the dialogue. Then answer this question: Who has Carmen's backpack?

B. Read the dialogue.

Maria's Teacher

Carmen: Excuse me, Maria. Is it okay if I borrow your calculator?

Maria: My what?

Carmen: Your calculator.

Maria: Oh, . . . this?

Carmen: Yes, that's a calculator.

Maria: Calculator.

Carmen: Right.

Maria: English words for math class are hard.

Carmen: Yeah, I know.

Maria: How do you say this in English?

Carmen: That's a protractor.

Maria: A protractor.

Carmen: That's right.

Maria: And this is a eraser, right?

Carmen: That's almost right. It's not *a* eraser. It's *an* eraser.

Maria: Oh, right. *An* eraser.

Carmen: This is fun. Wait . . . I have more things in my backpack.

Maria: Okay.

Carmen: Oh, no! This is not my backpack!

Maria: What?

Carmen: Look! These folders are not *my* folders! And I have a wallet with ten dollars in *my* backpack! And it's not here!

Maria: Ten dollars!?

Carmen:	Yes!
Maria:	Is it . . .
Carmen:	Wait! Here's a name . . . Carlos Alvarez!
Maria:	This is Carlos's backpack!
Carmen:	Yes . . . then Carlos has my backpack.
Maria:	And your ten dollars!

Pair Work

Read the dialogue with a classmate.

VOCABULARY

Words		Expressions
borrow	more	Excuse me, . . .
calculator	thing	Is it okay if . . .
hard	backpack	I know.
protractor	folder	How do you say this in (English)?
eraser	wallet	Oh, no!
fun	dollar	Look!
wait	here	

A. Read and say the vocabulary. Then write the vocabulary in your notebook.

B. Use word analysis to study the vocabulary (see page 250, Step 1).

C. Find the vocabulary in the dialogue. Then read the sentences that use the vocabulary.

D. Choose four words from the word box. In your notebook, write four sentences using these words.

Grammar 1

Articles: *a* and *an*

Use **a** before nouns that begin with consonant sounds.
Use **an** before nouns that begin with vowel sounds.

a	book comb hairbrush pencil wallet	**an**	apple eraser ice-cream bar orange umbrella

Vowels	Consonants
a, e, i, o, u	b, c, d, f, g, h, j, k, l, m, n, p, q, r, s, t, v, w, x, y, z

Remember: Sometimes *y* can make a vowel sound. For example, *my* and *very*.

Copy the sentences into your notebook. Then fill in the blanks with *a* or *an*.

1. Carmen has ____*an*____ umbrella.
2. Carlos has _____ backpack.
3. Mei has _____ orange.
4. Liliana has _____ notebook.
5. Samir has _____ eraser.

Demonstrative Pronouns: *this* and *that*

▲ This is an orange.   ▲ That is an apple.

that is = that's

A. Read the conversation. Then Listen.

A: Hi, Luis. Is this your backpack?

B: No, it's not. That's my backpack.

B. Practice the conversation in Exercise A with a classmate. Then make new conversations using your own information.

Grammar 2

Demonstrative Pronouns: *these* and *those*

▲ These are pens.　　　　▲ Those are erasers.

A. Look at the pictures. Then copy the sentences into your notebook.
Fill in the blanks with *these* or *those*.

1. *These* are pencils.

2. _____ are hairbrushes.

3. _____ are computers.

4. _____ are erasers.

5. _____ are umbrellas.

6. _____ are combs.

B. Copy the sentences into your notebook. Then fill in the blanks with *this,
that, these,* or *those.*

1. *Those* are folders.
(That / Those)

2. _____ is a comb.
(This / These)

3. _____ is an umbrella.
(This / These)

4. _____ is an orange.
(That / Those)

5. _____ are his pens.
(That / Those)

6. _____ are schedules.
(This / These)

Word Study

Short Vowel Sounds: /e/ and /u/

The letter *e* can stand for the short vowel sound /e/ as in *bed*.
The letter *u* can stand for the short vowel sound /u/ as in *cup*.

A. Use the learning strategy *Sound Out* (see page 32) and the pictures to read the words.

 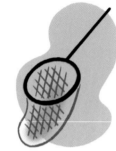  

1. pet   **2.** net   **3.** pen   **4.** ten

5. sun   **6.** bus   **7.** pup   **8.** run

B. Read the sentences aloud. Then copy them into your notebook. Circle the letters that stand for the short vowel sounds /e/ and /u/.

1. Mei has a new pup.   **4.** This is Pablo's pen.

2. Carmen and Carlos are on the bus.   **5.** Liliana has ten dollars.

3. Is that your pet?   **6.** It's hot in the sun.

C. Look at the dialogue on pages 38–39. Find one word with the short vowel sound /e/ and one word with the sound /u/. Write the words in your notebook.

Grammar 3

Possessive of Singular and Plural Nouns

▲ Keiko's pens

▲ Martin's backpack

▲ The girls' umbrellas

▲ The boys' caps

A. Copy the sentences into your notebook. Then fill in the blanks with the correct form of the possessive noun.

1. That is _Carlos's_ book. (Carlos)
2. That is _____ wallet. (Carmen)
3. This is _____ hairbrush. (Maria)
4. These are _____ pencils. (Bic)
5. Those are _____ notebooks. (Liliana)

B. Copy the sentences into your notebook. Then fill in the blanks with 's or '.

1. Pablo_'s_ wallet is from Mexico.
2. The boys_____ backpacks are big.
3. The students_____ schedules are the same.
4. My brother_____ name is Steve.
5. The students in Mr. Gomez_____ class speak English.

Reading

Preview the reading. Look at the picture of Carlos. What is he doing?
How does he feel? Talk about it with a classmate.

READ THIS!

Carlos's Backpack

Mr. Gomez has a backpack. It is a student's backpack. It has two
notebooks, a book, five pencils, two pens, three folders, a comb, and a
wallet. Mr. Gomez sees Carlos. Carlos is worried.

Mr. Gomez says, "Hi, Carlos. Are you okay?"

"Oh, hello, Mr. Gomez. No. I'm not okay. I have a big problem."

"A problem? What is it?" Mr. Gomez asks.

"It's my backpack, Mr. Gomez . . . Wait! *You* have my backpack!"

Mr. Gomez says, "So . . . is this *your* backpack?"

Carlos says, "Yes, it is."

"Then, what is in your backpack?" asks Mr. Gomez.

"Mr. Gomez, it's my backpack."

Mr. Gomez asks again. "Well, then, what is in your backpack?"

Carlos answers, "I have . . . a folder . . . no . . . I have three folders,
some pencils, two pens . . . oh, and my wallet is in my backpack, too!"

Mr. Gomez asks Carlos, "What is in your wallet?"

"I have eight dollars in my wallet, Mr. Gomez."

Mr. Gomez has a wallet. It is the wallet from the backpack. The wallet has ten dollars. It is not Carlos's wallet!

Mr. Gomez says, "Okay, Carlos. Is this your wallet?"

Carlos says, "Umm, no! It's not my wallet. That's my sister's wallet! Why is *her* wallet in *my* backpack?"

Mr. Gomez says, "Wait, Carlos. This is your sister's wallet. Is this your backpack or is it your sister's backpack?"

Carlos says, "Mr. Gomez, you're right! This isn't my backpack. It's my sister's backpack."

Mr. Gomez says, "Then Carmen has your backpack."

Carlos says, "Right. And Carmen has my wallet!"

AFTER YOU READ

A. Work in pairs to act out the story. Look at the story again. Read the words in quotation marks to act out the story about Carlos's backpack.

B. Fill in the blanks. In your notebook, write the correct word or words to complete each sentence.

  1. Mr. Gomez has *a student's* backpack.

    a. his brother's   **b.** a student's   **c.** Mrs. Garcia's

  2. Carlos is _____.

    a. happy   **b.** okay   **c.** worried

  3. Carlos has _____.

    a. an eraser   **b.** a problem   **c.** a calculator

  4. _____ wallet is in the backpack.

    a. Carlos's   **b.** Carmen's   **c.** Mr. Gomez's

Check your work. How many of your answers are correct? Write the number of correct answers in your notebook.

Keep Trying!   Great Work!

Writing

Tools for Writing

BEFORE YOU WRITE

A. You are going to write a paragraph about things in your backpack. First, read the paragraphs below.

> This is my backpack. I have a book, five pencils, two pens, and a wallet in my backpack. I have eight dollars in my wallet.
> This is my friend's backpack. She has three pencils, a calculator, a protractor, a folder, and an eraser. She also has a picture of her boyfriend in her backpack!

B. Read the *Before I Write* checklist. In your notebook, make a list of the things in your backpack and the things in your friend's backpack.

WRITE THIS!

Read the *While I Write* checklist. In your notebook, write one paragraph about what is in your backpack and one paragraph about what is in your friend's backpack. Ask your teacher for new words.

AFTER YOU WRITE

A. Read the *After I Write* checklist. Then check your work.

B. Read your paragraphs to a classmate. Then listen to your classmate read his or her paragraphs.

C. Write a final copy of your paragraphs in your notebook.

Before I Write

▶ Study the model.

▶ Think about things in backpacks.

▶ Make notes about . . .

   what is in my backpack

   what is in my friend's backpack

While I Write

▶ **Indent** the first line of each paragraph.

> This is my backpack. I have a book, five pencils, two pens . . .

▶ Use **a** before words that begin with consonant sounds. Use **an** before words that begin with vowel sounds.

   a wallet

   an eraser

▶ Use **number words** to tell *how many* things.

   eight dollars

After I Write

▶ Did I indent the first lines of my paragraphs?

▶ Did I use *a* before words that begin with consonant sounds and *an* before words that begin with vowel sounds?

▶ Did I use number words to tell how many things?

Learning Log

◆ VOCABULARY

Read the words and expressions. Then copy them into your notebook. Underline the words and expressions you need to review.

Nouns				Expressions
School Items		*Other*		Excuse me, . . .
backpack	folder	comb	thing	How do you say this
book	pencil	dollar	wallet	in (English)?
calculator	pen	fun		I know.
eraser	protractor	problem		Is it okay if . . .
Verbs	**Adjectives**		**Adverbs**	Look!
answer	big		again	Oh, no!
ask	hard		here	
borrow	more			
wait	some			
	worried			

◆ LANGUAGE and LEARNING STRATEGIES

Copy the checklist into your notebook. Check what you know. Review what you need to know.

I can . . .

_____ read and understand the dialogue "Maria's Teacher"

_____ use the articles *a* and *an* correctly

_____ use the demonstrative pronouns *this, that, these,* and *those* correctly

_____ form the possessive of singular and plural nouns

_____ read and use new words with the short vowel sounds /e/ and /u/

_____ use the learning strategy *Sound Out* to read new words

_____ read and understand the story "Carlos's Backpack"

_____ write a paragraph about the things in my backpack

◆ SELF-EVALUATION QUESTIONS

Answer the questions in your notebook.

1. What is easy in Chapter 3? What is difficult in Chapter 3?
2. How can you learn the things that are difficult?

UNIT **2** AT SCHOOL

GOALS
In Unit 2 you will learn to . . .

- listen to and read dialogues and stories about students at school

- ask and answer questions about where people, places, and things are

- use numbers from 1 to 100

- ask about personal information

- study words with consonant sounds

- fill out a form, write about places in your school, and write about your day

- use the learning strategies *Make Predictions* and *Use Selective Attention*

Chapter 4

Where's the gym?

Look at the picture. What things can you name in English? Say the words.

A. Listen to the dialogue. Then answer this question: Does Pablo have gym with Liliana?

B. Read the dialogue.

Lost at School

Pablo: Mei, where's the gym? I have P.E. in the gym.

Mei: The gym is downstairs.

Pablo: And where are the stairs?

Mei: Pablo! You aren't a new student! The stairs are next to Mr. Gomez's class. Go down the stairs. The gym is across from the cafeteria.

Pablo: Thank you, Mei.

★ ★ ★ ★ ★

Pablo: Hi, Liliana. I'm lost. I have P.E. in the gym. Where's the gym?

Liliana: I have P.E. now, too.

Pablo: That's great! Liliana, you're my best, best friend!

Liliana: Pablo, you're so silly!

Pablo: Ha! Ha! Okay, now, where's the gym?

Liliana: There's a gym in the building next to the . . .

Pablo: Hey, look. There's Samir. Hi, Samir!

Samir: Hi, Pablo. I have science now. What about you?

Pablo: I have P.E. with Liliana. See you at lunch.

Liliana: But . . . Pablo, . . . listen, . . . your P.E. class is in . . .

Pablo:	Liliana! This isn't my P.E. class!
Liliana:	I know! Your P.E. class is in the other gym.
Pablo:	The other gym! Are there two gyms in this school?
Liliana:	Well . . . no . . .
Pablo:	No?
Liliana:	No . . . there are three gyms!
Pablo:	Three gyms . . . great.
Liliana:	It's a big school! Ha! Ha! Ha!

Pair and Group Work

A. Read the dialogue with a classmate.

B. Act out the dialogue in groups of four.

VOCABULARY

Words		Expressions
gym	lost	What about you?
downstairs	best	See you (at lunch).
stairs	so	
next to	silly	
go	building	
across from	listen	
cafeteria	other	

A. Read and say the vocabulary. Then write the vocabulary in your notebook.

B. Use word analysis to study the vocabulary (see page 250, Steps 1–2).

C. Find the vocabulary in the dialogue. Then read the sentences that use the vocabulary.

D. Choose five words from the word box. In your notebook, write five sentences using these words.

Grammar 1

Prepositions of Location: *in, on, under, next to*

▲ The turtle is in the box. ▲ The turtle is on the box.

▲ The turtle is under the box. ▲ The turtle is next to the box.

Copy the sentences into your notebook. Then fill in the blanks with *in, on, under,* or *next to.*

1. The folder is
   ___*under*___ the book.

2. The eraser is
   _____ the pencil.

3. The calculator is
   _____ the book.

4. The notebook is
   _____ the backpack.

5. The binder is
   _____ the backpack.

6. The pen is
   _____ the folder.

Grammar 2

Where Questions with *be*

Where	am	I?	You are		
	are	you?	I am		
	is	he? she? it?	He is She is It is	in the gym.	
	are	we? you? they?	You are We are They are		

where is = where's

A. Copy the questions into your notebook. Then fill in the blanks with the correct form of the verb *be*.

1. Where ___*are*___ the stairs?
2. Where _____ the cafeteria?
3. Where _____ Maria and Bic?
4. Where _____ Carlos?
5. Where _____ Mei?

B. Tell about your school. Read the questions. Then write your answers in your notebook. Choose expressions from the box, or use your own.

EXAMPLE: Where's your math class?
   It's in room 135.

> in the other building
> across from the (gym)
> in room (406)
> next to the (library)

1. Where's the library?
2. Where's the gym?
3. Where's your science class?
4. Where's your English class?
5. Where's the cafeteria?

Word Study

Consonant Sounds: /ch/ and /sh/

The letters *ch* can stand for the consonant sound /ch/ as in *lunch*.
The letters *sh* can stand for the consonant sound /sh/ as in *English*.

A. Use the learning strategy *Sound Out* (see page 32) and the pictures to read the words.

1. chin   **2.** bench   **3.** lunch   **4.** inch

5. ship   **6.** shut   **7.** fish   **8.** dish

B. Read the sentences aloud. Then copy them into your notebook. Circle the letters that stand for the consonant sounds /ch/ and /sh/.

1. Where is your lunch?   **4.** Carmen's hat is on the bench.

2. Please shut the door.   **5.** Are they on that ship?

3. That is a very pretty dish.   **6.** Does Bic have two fish?

C. Look at Exercise A. Choose two words with the consonant sound /ch/ and two words with the consonant sound /sh/. In your notebook, write a sentence for each word.

Grammar 3

There is and there are

There is	a teacher	in the room.	There are	two teachers	in the gym.
	one teacher			ten teachers	
	a girl			many people	
	one girl			some students	
Remember: Use *there is* before a singular noun. Use *there are* before a plural noun.					

> there is = there's

A. Copy the sentences into your notebook. Then fill in the blanks with *there is* or *there are*.

1. *There are* nine girls in this class.
2. _____ one art teacher at this school.
3. _____ a new student in Mrs. Kim's class.
4. _____ many books in my backpack.
5. _____ two pencils on the desk.

B. In your notebook, write three sentences about your class and three sentences about your school. Use *there's* and *there are*.

EXAMPLE: *There's a library across from the gym.*
There are two computers in our class.

C. Look at the picture. Write five sentences about the picture. Use *in*, *on*, and *next to* in your sentences.

EXAMPLE: *There are three books on the desk.*

Reading

Use the learning strategy *Make Predictions*.

1. Look at the pictures and the title.
2. Look for words you know in the story.
3. What do you think the story is about?
4. Make a prediction.
5. Tell your prediction to your classmates.

READ THIS!

I Love School!

Hi! My name is Liliana. I am sixteen years old. I come from Peru. I live in the United States. I am a student. I go to Washington School. Where is Washington School? It is on School Street.

Washington School is a nice school. There are many classrooms, and there are many teachers. There are three gyms and a big auditorium. The cafeteria is nice. It is across from one of the gyms. There are many tables and chairs in the cafeteria. There is a library with a lot of books. The library has a lot of computers, too. I use the computers in the library every day. I really like computers.

I have seven classes this year. I have art, history, English, P.E., math, science, and music. I have English with Mr. Gomez. There are fifteen students in my English class. My science class is big. There are twenty students in my science class. My math class is small. In my math class, there are nine students. I like math and science. I like English, too. I like all my classes. I love school. I am a good student. And I go to a great school!

AFTER YOU READ

A. Think about the learning strategy. What predictions did you make about the story before you read it? Were your predictions correct? As you read the story, did you need to change your predictions? What information or clues did you use to make your predictions? Discuss your answers with a classmate.

B. True or false? In your notebook, write *True* or *False* for each statement. For your *False* statements, make the sentences correct.

EXAMPLE: Liliana is a teacher. *False. Liliana is a student.*

1. Liliana likes computers.
2. One of the gyms is across from the cafeteria.
3. Liliana is seventeen years old.
4. Liliana doesn't like P.E.
5. There are many students in Liliana's science class.

Check your work. How many of your answers are correct? Write the number of correct answers in your notebook.

Keep Trying!   Great Work!

Writing

A. You are going to write a paragraph about places in your school. First, read the paragraph below.

> My name is Liliana. I go to Washington School. Washington School has a cafeteria and three gyms. There are many classrooms in my school and there is a big library. The library is my favorite place in school. The library has many books and computers. I like to use the computers in the library.

B. Read the *Before I Write* checklist. In your notebook, make a list of the places in your school. Choose a favorite place. Make notes about that place.

WRITE THIS!

Read the *While I Write* checklist. Look at your notes and write a paragraph about your school. Ask your teacher for new words.

AFTER YOU WRITE

A. Read the *After I Write* checklist. Then check your work.

B. Read your paragraph to a classmate. Then listen to your classmate read his or her paragraph.

C. Write a final copy of your paragraph in your notebook.

Tools for Writing

Before I Write

▶ Study the model.

▶ Think about places in my school.

▶ Make notes about . . .

  my favorite place in school

  where that place is

  what that place has

  what I do there

While I Write

▶ Use **has / have** and **there is / there are** to tell about places in my school.

> Washington School has a cafeteria and three gyms.
>
> There is a big library.

▶ Use location words like **in**, **next to**, or **across from** to tell where places are.

> There are many classrooms in my school.

After I Write

▶ Did I use *has / have* and *there is / there are* to tell about places in my school?

▶ Did I use location words like *in*, *next to*, or *across from* to tell where places are?

Learning Log

◆ VOCABULARY

Read the words and expressions. Then copy them into your notebook. Underline the words and expressions you need to review.

Nouns				Expressions
Rooms in School		***Other***		I come from (Peru).
auditorium	gym	building	stairs	See you (at lunch).
cafeteria	library	chair	table	What about you?
classroom				

Verbs		Adjectives		Adverbs	Question Word
go	live	a lot of	other	downstairs	where
like	use	best	silly	so	
listen		lost	small		
		nice			

◆ LANGUAGE and LEARNING STRATEGIES

Copy the checklist into your notebook. Check what you know. Review what you need to know.

I can . . .

_____ read and understand the dialogue "Lost at School"

_____ ask and answer questions about where someone or something is

_____ use *there is* and *there are* correctly

_____ read and use new words with the consonant sounds /ch/ and /sh/

_____ use the learning strategy *Make Predictions* to guess what a story will be about

_____ read and understand the story "I Love School!"

_____ write a paragraph about places in my school

◆ SELF-EVALUATION QUESTIONS

Answer the questions in your notebook.

1. What is easy in Chapter 4? What is difficult in Chapter 4?
2. How can you learn the things that are difficult?

Chapter 5

What's your address?

GETTING READY

Look at the picture. What things can you name in English? Say the words.

LISTENING AND READING

A. Listen to the dialogue. Then answer this question: Who is having a party?

B. Read the dialogue.

The Party

Liliana: Do you know what? This Saturday, there's a party at Carmen and Carlos's house.

Samir: There is? Can I come?

Liliana: I don't know. Here come Carmen and Carlos now. You can ask them.

★ ★ ★ ★ ★

Samir: Hey! Can I come to your party?

Carmen: Sure! All of you can come.

Pablo: Where's the party?

Carlos: At our house.

Liliana: What's your address?

Carlos: Our address is 316 Fifth Street.

Pablo: Where's that? I need directions.

Liliana: Yeah, and he needs directions to the gym, too. Right, Pablo?

Pablo: Ha, ha, ha . . . very funny, Liliana.

Carmen: Hey, Pablo. Do you want a map to our house?

Carlos: Come on, Carmen. Pablo doesn't need a map. Pablo, do you know where the fire station is?

Pablo: Yes, I do.

Carlos: There's a building across from the fire station. It's white and green. We live next to that building.

Carmen: Okay, Pablo? Can you find it?

Pablo: Um . . . maybe . . . What's your phone number?

Carmen: It's 555-2377.

Liliana:	Don't worry, Pablo. We can go to the party together.
Pablo:	Okay, Liliana. Thanks.
Carlos:	Oh, hi, Maria! Can you come to our party on Saturday?
Maria:	No, I'm sorry. I can't.
Carmen:	Oh, Maria, please come to our party!
Maria:	I'm sorry. I cannot come.

 **Pair and Group Work**

A. Read the dialogue with a classmate.

B. Act out the dialogue in groups of six.

VOCABULARY

Words		Expressions
party	want	Do you know what?
house	map	Sure!
come	fire station	Come on.
all	find	Don't worry.
address	maybe	I'm sorry.
directions	phone number	
funny	please	
need		

A. Read and say the vocabulary. Then write the vocabulary in your notebook.

B. Use word analysis to study the vocabulary (see page 250, Steps 1–2).

C. Find the vocabulary in the dialogue. Then read the sentences that use the vocabulary.

D. Work with a classmate. Choose a word from the word box and draw a picture of it. Don't speak. Your classmate has to guess which word you are drawing. Take turns.

Grammar 1

What Questions with *be*

What	is	that?	It is a map.
		her address?	Her address is 316 Fifth Street.
	are	their names?	Their names are Samir and Mei.
		your favorite classes?	My favorite classes are art and math.

what is = what's

A. Write the numbers 1–5 in your notebook. Match each question in the left-hand column with an answer from the right-hand column. Write the letter of the correct answer in your notebook.

_e_ **1.** What's your address?   **a.** They're my sister's books.

____ **2.** What are those?   **b.** It's 555-2139.

____ **3.** What's his phone number?   **c.** It's my schedule.

____ **4.** What's this?   **d.** Their names are Rosa and Bill.

____ **5.** What are their names?   **e.** It's 872 Whitehall Avenue.

B. Read the conversation. Then listen.

A: What's your favorite class?

B: It's U.S. history.

A: What's the teacher's name?

B: Her name is Mrs. Jackson.

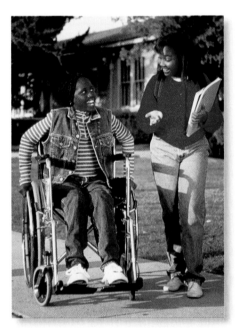

C. Practice the conversation in Exercise B with a classmate. Then make new conversations using your own information.

☀ Check your Vocabulary Handbook (page 232) for other school subjects.

Grammar 2

Present Tense of Regular Verbs: Statements

Affirmative Statements			Negative Statements		
I You	**need**		I You	**do not** need	
He/She	**needs**	a map.	He/She	**does not** need	a map.
We You They	**need**		We You They	**do not** need	

do not	= don't
does not	= doesn't

Copy the sentences into your notebook.
Then fill in the blanks with the correct
form of the verb.

1. Maria _speaks_ Spanish. (speak / speaks)
2. Carlos and Carmen _____ on Fifth Street. (live / lives)
3. Liliana _____ a new backpack. (want / wants)
4. Mr. Gomez _____ Vietnamese. (don't speak / doesn't speak)
5. We _____ tests. (don't like / doesn't like)

Present Tense of Regular Verbs: *Yes/No* Questions

Do	I you				you I	**do.**		you I	**don't.**
Does	he/she	**need**	a map?	Yes,	he/she	**does.**	No,	he/she	**doesn't.**
Do	we you they				you we they	**do.**		you we they	**don't.**

In your notebook, write three *yes/no* questions. Use the verbs *speak*,
like, and *need*. Then ask a classmate your questions. Answer your
classmate's questions.

EXAMPLE: *Do you need directions to the cafeteria?*
No, I don't.

Word Study

Consonant Blends

Consonant blends are two consonants that come together in a word. Sometimes they come at the beginning of a word. You can hear the sounds of both letters in the blend.

EXAMPLES: **cl**ass   **pr**etty   **st**udent

A. Use the learning strategy *Sound Out* (see page 32) and the pictures to read the words.

1. dress

2. black

3. clock

4. drum

5. swim

6. flag

7. class

8. glass

B. Read the sentences aloud. Then copy them into your notebook. Circle the consonant blends that come at the beginning of a word.

1. I have a red dress for the party.
2. Sam can play the drums.
3. Pablo swims after school every day.
4. Do you need black pants?
5. We have a flag in our class.
6. She doesn't need a new clock.

C. Look at Exercise A. Choose two words with consonant blends that come at the beginning of a word. In your notebook, write a sentence for each word.

Grammar 3

Statements with *can*

Affirmative Statements			Negative Statements		
I You He/She We You They	**can** come	to the party.	I You He/She We You They	**cannot** come	to the party.

cannot = can't

Copy the sentences into your notebook. Then fill in the
blanks with *can* or *can't*.

1. Maria ___can't___ come to the party. (negative)
2. Liliana and Mei _____ come to the party. (affirmative)
3. Pablo _____ play the drums. (negative)
4. Carmen and Carlos _____ swim. (affirmative)
5. We _____ speak Chinese. (negative)

Yes/No Questions with *can*

Can	I you he/she we you they	come to the party?	Yes,	you I he/she you we they	**can.**	No,	you I he/she you we they	**can't.**

A. Copy the sentences into your notebook. Change each statement to a question.
Write the questions in your notebook.

1. You can answer this question. *Can you answer this question?*
2. Bic can speak English and Chinese.
3. Samir and Liliana can come to the party.
4. We can play the drums.
5. It can swim.

B. In your notebook, write five *yes/no* questions with *can*. Then ask a classmate
your questions. Answer your classmate's questions.

EXAMPLE: *Can you speak Chinese?*

Reading

As you read, use the learning strategy *Use Selective Attention* to answer this question: Why can't Maria go to the party on Saturday?

READ THIS!

Use Selective Attention
When you *Use Selective Attention,* you focus on key ideas and words. Focusing on the important information will help you to ignore distractions and understand what you read.

Maria's Job

Maria cannot go to the party on Saturday. She is not happy.

Carmen says, "Please come to our party, Maria."

"I can't," says Maria sadly.

"Come on, Maria. A party is fun!" Carlos says."

"I'm sorry, Carlos."

Carlos says, "But Maria! We can eat great enchiladas at the party!"

"And we can dance," Samir says.

"And we can eat great enchiladas!" Carlos says again.

Carmen says, "Seriously, Maria, we can have a lot of fun."

Carlos says, "And we can eat great . . . !"

"I know . . ." Maria says. "We can eat great enchiladas. But I can't. I have a job on Saturday."

Samir asks Maria about her job. She baby-sits three children on Saturdays.

"That's a good job," says Samir.

"Yes, it is," says Maria. "I love my job. I love children."

Samir says, "Yes, children are great. I baby-sit my little brothers and sister."

Carmen says, "Wow . . . I need a job. But I don't need a hard job. I don't have a lot of time. But I do need money for CDs."

"I'm sorry you can't come to the party," says Samir to Maria.

"I'm sorry, too," says Maria.

"You can't come to the party?" asks Carlos.

Samir, Carmen, and Maria look at Carlos.

"What?" asks Carlos. "Um . . . well . . . seriously, Maria, the enchiladas really aren't very good. You know . . . I'm the enchilada chef . . . and . . ."

"And," says Carmen, "he still needs a lot of practice!"

They laugh. But Maria is still sad. She cannot go to their party.

AFTER YOU READ

A. Did you use the learning strategy *Use Selective Attention* to find the answer to the question in *Before You Read*? Find the sentence in the story that answers the question. Discuss your answer with a classmate.

B. True or false? In your notebook, write *True* or *False* for each statement. Write *I don't know* if the information is *not* in the reading.

1. Maria can go to the party on Saturday.
2. Carlos says, "A job is fun."
3. Maria loves baby-sitting.
4. Samir has brothers and a sister.
5. Maria's job is at night.

Check your work. How many of your answers are correct? Write the number of correct answers in your notebook.

Writing

BEFORE YOU WRITE

A. You are going to fill out a form with your personal information. First, read the form below.

PERSONAL INFORMATION FORM

Name _____Lopez_____ _____Maria_____
           Last name   **First name**

Address _____42 Walnut St., Apt. 3H_____
                              Street
           Houston, TX   _77027_
           City and state   **Zip code**

Home telephone ___(713)___   ___555-9813___
                      Area code   **Number**

Name of parent or guardian ___Lopez___   ___Marta___
                                  Last name   **First name**

Parent or guardian's work telephone
   _(713)_   _555-6412_
Area code   **Number**

B. Read the *Before I Write* checklist. Write the personal information about yourself in your notebook.

WRITE THIS!

Copy the printed part of the form in your notebook. Use the *While I Write* checklist to help you fill in the form correctly. Ask your teacher for help with spelling and abbreviations.

AFTER YOU WRITE

A. Read the *After I Write* checklist. Then check your use of capitalization, spelling, and abbreviations.

B. Read the information on your form to a classmate. Then listen to your classmate read his or her form.

C. Write a final copy of your form in your notebook.

Before I Write

▶ Study the model.

▶ Find the information I need.

▶ Write down correct . . .
   names
   address
   phone numbers

While I Write

▶ Put a **capital letter** at the beginning of the names of people, streets, and cities.

   Lopez, Maria

▶ Use the abbreviation **St.** for **Street** and **Apt.** for **Apartment**.

   42 Walnut St., Apt. 3H

▶ Use **abbreviations** for the names of states. Put state abbreviations in all **capital letters**.

   Houston, TX 77027

After I Write

▶ Did I put a capital letter at the beginning of the names of people, streets, and cities?

▶ Did I use the abbreviation *St.* for *Street* and *Apt.* for *Apartment*?

▶ Did I use abbreviations for the names of states?

Learning Log

◆ VOCABULARY

Read the words and expressions. Then copy them in your notebook. Underline the words and expressions you need to review.

Nouns				Expressions
People	**Other**			Come on.
chef	address	fire station	phone number	Do you know what?
children	directions	map	practice	Don't worry.
	house	money	time	I'm sorry.
	job	party		Sure!

Verbs		Adjectives		Adverbs	
baby-sit	eat	all	little	about	sadly
can	find	funny	sad	maybe	seriously
come	need	happy		please	still
dance	want			really	

◆ LANGUAGE and LEARNING STRATEGIES

Copy the checklist into your notebook. Check what you know. Review what you need to know.

I can . . .

_____ read and understand the dialogue "The Party"

_____ ask and answer questions with *what*

_____ ask and answer questions using the present tense

_____ ask and answer questions using *can*

_____ read and use new words with consonant blends such as *class*

_____ use the learning strategy *Use Selective Attention* to find key ideas before I read

_____ read and understand the story "Maria's Job"

_____ complete a personal information form

◆ SELF-EVALUATION QUESTIONS

Answer the questions in your notebook.

1. What is easy in Chapter 5? What is difficult in Chapter 5?
2. How can you learn the things that are difficult?

Chapter 6

You were late yesterday.

Look at the picture. What things can you name in English? Say the words.

A. Listen to the dialogue. Then answer this question: What time does class start?

B. Read the dialogue.

Late Again

Mr. Gomez: Where's Carmen? Is she sick today, Carlos?

Carlos: No, Mr. Gomez. She isn't sick. She's in school today.

Mr. Gomez: Well, we can't wait for her. Please take out a piece of paper and . . . well . . . good morning, Carmen . . .

Carmen: Oh, uh . . . good morning.

Mr. Gomez: Do you know what time it is?

Carmen: Yes, . . . I do. It's ten minutes after ten.

Mr. Gomez: Really? And does class start at ten minutes after ten?

Carmen: No. It starts at ten o'clock.

Mr. Gomez: It does?

Carmen: I'm sorry we're late . . .

Mr. Gomez: Yes, Carmen, you're late again.

Carmen: I'm really sorry! I was with a new student. Here she is. Her name is Sophie. She was in the hall. She was . . .

Mr. Gomez: Thank you, Carmen. But you're still late for class today. And you were ten minutes late to class yesterday.

Carmen: Yes, Mr. Gomez.

* * * * *

Mr. Gomez: So, where are you from, Sophie?

Sophie:	Haiti.
Mr. Gomez:	And what other languages do you speak?
Sophie:	I speak Haitian Creole and French.
Mr. Gomez:	That's great! Sophie, please sit here. Oh . . . and, Carmen, . . . when does class start?
Carmen:	Ten o'clock, Mr. Gomez.

Pair and Group Work

A. Read the dialogue with a classmate.

B. Act out the dialogue in groups of four.

VOCABULARY

Words		Expressions
sick	hall	Really?
today	yesterday	So, . . .
take out	Haiti	
piece	Haitian Creole	
paper	French	
start	sit	
late		

A. Read and say the vocabulary. Then write the vocabulary in your notebook.

B. Use word analysis to study the vocabulary (see page 250, Steps 1–2).

C. Find the vocabulary in the dialogue. Then read the sentences that use the vocabulary.

D. Choose five of the words from the word box. In your notebook, write a mini-dialogue using these words. Practice your dialogue with a classmate.

Grammar 1

What Questions with do

What	do	I you	need?	You I	need	a piece of paper.
	does	he/she		He/She	needs	
	do	we you they		You We They	need	

A. Copy the questions and answers into your notebook. Fill in the blanks with the correct form of *do* and the correct form of the regular verbs.

1. What ___do___ Carlos and Pablo like? They ___like___ P.E.
2. What _____ you need? We _____ a piece of paper.
3. What _____ Carmen like? She _____ math.
4. What _____ they want? They _____ a pet.
5. What _____ you have? I _____ a pencil.

B. Read each answer. Write the question it responds to in your notebook.

1. He has a calculator. (Samir) *What does Samir have?*
2. They need a piece of paper. (the students)
3. He needs a new wallet. (Mr. Gomez)
4. I have a new backpack. (you)
5. We need directions. (you)

Grammar 2

What + Noun

What	language	do	I you	speak?	You I	speak	French.
		does	he/she		He/She	speaks	
		do	we you they		You We They	speak	

A. Write the numbers 1–5 in your notebook. Match each phrase in the left-hand column with a phrase from the right-hand column. Write the complete sentences in your notebook.

EXAMPLE: *What color do you like?*

1. What color
2. What time
3. What languages
4. What class
5. What books

a. does she have after math?
b. do I have in my backpack?
c. do you like?
d. do you eat lunch?
e. do they speak?

B. Read the conversation. Then listen.

A: What time do you eat lunch?

B: I eat lunch at twelve o'clock.

C. Practice the conversation in Exercise B with a classmate. Then make new conversations using your own information.

Check your Vocabulary Handbook (page 227) for other daily activities.

Word Study

Consonant Blends

Sometimes consonant blends come at the end of a word. You can hear the sounds of both letters in the blend.

EXAMPLES: fi**nd**   wa**nt**   be**st**

A. Use the learning strategy *Sound Out* (see page 32) and the pictures to read the words.

1. gift   **2.** mask   **3.** belt   **4.** hand

5. lamp   **6.** plant   **7.** tent   **8.** stamp

B. Read the sentences aloud. Then copy them into your notebook. Circle the consonant blends that come at the end of a word.

1. Where is my red belt?   **4.** That is a pretty plant!

2. I don't have a gift for Carlos.   **5.** Do you have my mask?

3. Do you like this lamp?   **6.** My mother can't find a stamp.

C. Look at Exercise A. Choose three words with consonant blends that come at the end of a word. In your notebook, write a sentence for each word.

Grammar 3

Past Tense of *be*: Statements

Affirmative Statements			Negative Statements		
I	**was**		I	**was not**	
You	**were**		You	**were not**	
He/She	**was**	late yesterday.	He/She	**was not**	late yesterday.
We			We		
You	**were**		You	**were not**	
They			They		

was not = wasn't
were not = weren't

A. Change each statement from affirmative to negative. Write the new sentences in your notebook. Use *wasn't* or *weren't*.

1. Carmen was late to class. *Carmen wasn't late to class.*
2. We were with a new student.
3. Liliana and Mei were in school yesterday.

B. Change each statement from negative to affirmative. Write the new sentences in your notebook.

1. Pablo wasn't sick yesterday. *Pablo was sick yesterday.*
2. Maria wasn't in English class.
3. Carlos and Bic weren't at lunch.

Past Tense of *be*: Yes/No Questions

Was	I				you	**were.**		you	**weren't.**
Were	you				I	**was.**		I	**wasn't.**
Was	he/she	late yesterday?	Yes,	he/she	**was.**	No,	he/she	**wasn't.**
	we			you			you	
Were	you			we	**were.**		we	**weren't.**
	they			they			they	

Write five *yes/no* questions with the past tense of *be* in your notebook. Then ask a classmate your questions. Answer your classmate's questions.

EXAMPLE: *Was Annan sick yesterday?*
No, he wasn't.

Reading

BEFORE YOU READ

Use the learning strategy *Make Predictions* (see page 56).

1. Look at the picture and the title of the story.
2. Look for words you know in the story.
3. What do you think the story is about?
4. Make a prediction.
5. Tell your prediction to your classmates.

READ THIS!

My Journal

Monday

Today I was late for English. It was five minutes after ten. Mr. Gomez wasn't angry.

Today I was also late for math. It was ten minutes after one. Mrs. Garcia was angry. There's a math test Tuesday. That's tomorrow! But I'm not nervous. I'm pretty good at math.

Tuesday

Today I was early for math. Mrs. Garcia was very happy. The math test was easy. After the math test, I was very happy!

Today I was late for English again. It was ten minutes after ten. Mr. Gomez was not angry yesterday. Today, he was angry. Can I be on time for English tomorrow? There's an English test tomorrow. Now, I'm nervous! English tests are hard.

Wednesday

Today was a very bad day. I was late for math, and I was late for English. Mr. Gomez was very, very angry. The English test was very, very hard.

What is my problem? I am late to class almost every day. I know! I don't have a watch! I want a watch for my birthday.

AFTER YOU READ

A. Think about the learning strategy. What predictions did you make about the story before you read it? Were your predictions correct? As you read the story, did you need to change your predictions? What information or clues did you use to make your predictions? Discuss your answers with a classmate.

B. Fill in the blanks. In your notebook, write the correct word to complete each sentence.

1. Carmen's math test was _____.
   a. hard   **b.** easy   **c.** silly
2. On Tuesday, Carmen was late for _____.
   a. math   **b.** P.E.   **c.** English
3. On Wednesday, Carmen was _____ for English and math.
   a. early   **b.** late   **c.** on time
4. On Wednesday, Mr. Gomez was _____.
   a. angry   **b.** worried   **c.** happy

Check your work. How many of your answers are correct? Write the number of correct answers in your notebook.

Keep Trying!   Great Work!

Writing

BEFORE YOU WRITE

A. You are going to write a paragraph in your journal about your day yesterday. First, read the paragraph from a student's journal below.

> Wednesday
>
> Yesterday was a bad day. My sister was ten minutes late for English class. She was with a new student in the hall. They were both late. Mr. Gomez was angry. I was five minutes late for math class. There was a math test. It was very hard. I was nervous. I'm not a good student in math. What can I do? I can study more.

B. Read the *Before I Write* checklist. In your notebook, make notes about what you did yesterday and how you felt.

WRITE THIS!

Read the *While I Write* checklist. Look at your notes and write a paragraph about your day yesterday. Ask your teacher for new words.

AFTER YOU WRITE

A. Read the *After I Write* checklist. Then check your work.

B. Read your paragraph to a classmate. Then listen to your classmate read his or her paragraph.

C. Write a final copy of your paragraph in your notebook.

Before I Write

▶ Study the model.

▶ Think about my day yesterday.

▶ Make notes about . . .
  what I did
  how I felt

While I Write

▶ Use **describing words** to tell how you felt.

  I was nervous.

▶ Use **was** and **were** to write about the past.

  Mr. Gomez was angry.

▶ Give **details** about time and place.

  My sister was ten minutes late for English class.

After I Write

▶ Did I use describing words to tell how I felt?

▶ Did I use *was* and *were* to write about the past?

▶ Did I give details about time and place?

Learning Log

◆ VOCABULARY

Read the words and expressions. Then copy them into your notebook.
Underline the words and expressions you need to review.

Nouns					Expressions
Country	**Languages**	**Time Words**	**Other**		I'm pretty good at (math).
Haiti	French	today	birthday	piece	Really?
	Haitian Creole	tomorrow	hall	test	So, . . .
		yesterday	minutes	watch	on time
			paper		
Verbs		**Adjectives**		**Question Word**	
sit take out		angry hard		when	
start		bad late			
		early sick			
		easy			

◆ LANGUAGE and LEARNING STRATEGIES

Copy the checklist into your notebook. Check what you know. Review what you
need to know.

I can . . .

_____ read and understand the dialogue "Late Again"

_____ ask and tell what time I do different activities

_____ ask and answer questions with *what*

_____ ask and answer questions using the past tense of *be*

_____ read and use new words with consonant blends such as *find*

_____ use the learning strategy *Make Predictions* to guess what a story
will be about

_____ read and understand the story "My Journal"

_____ write a journal entry about my day yesterday

◆ SELF-EVALUATION QUESTIONS

Answer the questions in your notebook.

1. What is easy in Chapter 6? What is difficult in Chapter 6?
2. How can you learn the things that are difficult?

UNIT **3** AT HOME

GOALS
In Unit 3 you will learn to . . .

- listen to and read dialogues and stories about activities at home and at a party

- describe what you usually do and what you are doing now

- ask and answer questions about activities and preferences

- study words with long vowel sounds

- write about your activities, write about a classmate, and write a letter to a friend

- use the learning strategies *Make Predictions, Use What You Know,* and *Make Inferences*

81

Chapter 7

What are you doing?

GETTING READY

Look at the picture. What things can you name in English? Say the words. Make sentences about what you see and what the people are doing.

LISTENING AND READING

A. Listen to the dialogue. Then answer this question: Who is Carolina?

B. Read the dialogue.

Help for Carlos

Carlos: Oh, no! Carmen, where are you?

Carmen: I'm in the bedroom.

Carlos: Please help me.

Carmen: I can't help you right now. I'm making the bed.

Carlos: David, what are you doing? I need help.

David: I can't help you right now. I'm cleaning the windows. Ask Mom.

Mother: I'm busy, Carlos.

Carlos: Oh, no! I need help. Carolina, where are you? What are you doing? Please come and help me!

Father: Carlos, your sister is busy. She can't help you now. She's washing her hair.

Carlos: Dad, I need help! I mean . . . I need help *now*!

Father: Carlos, just calm down. I can't come now. I'm busy changing a lightbulb. What *are* you doing?

Carlos: I'm cooking!

Father: Oh, dear! Ask Grandma. She can help you.

Carlos: Grandma . . . ?

Grandmother: Carlos, I'm coming. Where are you?

Carlos: I'm in the kitchen, Grandma. Please help me.

Grandmother: Oh, Carlos, you're burning the sauce!

Carlos: I know, Grandma!

Grandmother: Well, turn off the stove! Now!

Pair and Group Work

A. Read the dialogue with a classmate.

B. Act out the dialogue in groups of five.

VOCABULARY

Words		Expressions
bedroom	cook	right now
help	kitchen	I mean . . .
make the bed	burn	calm down
clean the window	sauce	Oh, dear!
busy	turn off	
wash her hair	stove	
change a lightbulb		

A. Read and say the vocabulary. Then write the vocabulary in your notebook.

B. Use word analysis to study the vocabulary (see page 250, Steps 1–2).

C. Find the vocabulary in the dialogue. Then read the sentences that use the vocabulary.

D. Group words that go together. Write these headings in your notebook: Verbs; Family Names; Rooms in a House; Things in a House; Other Words. Find the new words in the dialogue that go in each of these groups. Write them in your notebook.

Grammar 1

Present Continuous Tense: Statements

I	am				the bed.
You	are				
He/She	is	(not)	making		
We					
You	are				
They					

clean	→	cleaning
get	→	getting
write	→	writing

is not	=	isn't
are not	=	aren't

A. Copy the sentences into your notebook. Then fill in the blanks with the correct form of the verb.

1. She ___is eating___ lunch. (eat)

2. We _____ in our notebooks. (write)

3. He _____ his hair. (wash)

4. They _____ the classroom. (clean)

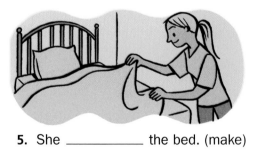

5. She _____ the bed. (make)

6. They _____ ready for school. (get)

B. Rewrite the sentences in Exercise A. Use *isn't* or *aren't*.

EXAMPLE: *She isn't eating lunch.*

Grammar 2

Present Continuous Tense: *What* Questions

What	am	I	cooking?	You	are	cooking	enchiladas.
	are	you		I	am		
	is	he/she		He/She	is		
		we		You			
	are	you		We	are		
		they		They			

what is = what's

Read each answer. Write the question it responds to in your notebook. Use *what's* or *what are*.

1. She's reading a history book. (Liliana) *What's Liliana reading?*
2. He's cleaning the windows. (David)
3. They're making enchiladas. (Mom and Dad)
4. I'm eating lunch. (you)
5. We're studying math. (you)

Present Continuous Tense: *Yes/No* Questions

Am	I	studying?	Yes,	you	are.	No,	you	aren't.
Are	you			I	am.		I'm not.	
Is	he/she			he/she	is.		he/she	isn't.
	we			you			you	
Are	you			we	are.		we	aren't.
	they			they			they	

A. Read the conversation. Then listen.

A: What are you doing?

B: I'm helping my sister.

A: Oh. Is she studying?

B: No, she isn't. She's making cookies.

B. Practice the conversation in Exercise A with a classmate. Then make new conversations using other phrases.

Word Study

Long Vowel Sounds: /ā/, /ī/, /ō/, /yōo/

The letters *a_e* can stand for the long vowel sound /ā/ as in *came*.

The letters *i_e* can stand for the long vowel sound /ī/ as in *like*.

The letters *o_e* can stand for the long vowel sound /ō/ as in *close*.

The letters *u_e* can stand for the long vowel sound /yōo/ as in *use*.

The last letter of each word is *e*. You do not hear it. The vowel before the final, silent *e* is usually long.

A. Use the learning strategy *Sound Out* (see page 32) and the pictures to read the words.

1. cake   **2.** page   **3.** five   **4.** bike

5. rose   **6.** nose   **7.** cute   **8.** cube

B. Read the sentences aloud. Then copy them into your notebook. Circle the letters that stand for the long vowel sounds /ā/, /ī/, /ō/, and /yōo/.

1. That dress is very cute!

2. Does Anna have five dollars?

3. Jan is eating cake.

4. Please turn to page ten in your books.

5. Where is Samir's bike?

6. Kevin has a rose for Kelly.

C. Look at Exercise A. Choose one word for each of these long vowel sounds: /ā/, /ī/, /ō/, and /yōo/. In your notebook, write a sentence for each word.

Grammar 3

Object Pronouns

An **object pronoun** replaces a noun in the object position.		
Grandma	is helping	**me.** **you.** **him.** / **her.** **it.** **us.** **you.** **them.**
Remember: Use an object pronoun after the verb in a sentence.		

Subject Pronouns		Object Pronouns
I	⟶	**me**
you	⟶	**you**
he	⟶	**him**
she	⟶	**her**
it	⟶	**it**
we	⟶	**us**
you	⟶	**you**
they	⟶	**them**

A. Copy the sentences into your notebook. Fill in the blanks with the correct object pronoun.

1. She is drying ___*them*___. (the dishes)
2. We are helping _____. (Mom)
3. Carlos is burning _____. (the sauce)
4. Dad is eating _____. (a cookie)
5. Grandma is helping _____. (I)

B. Look at the sentences in Exercise A. In your notebook, write *yes/no* questions for these sentences. Use object pronouns. Then write short answers.

EXAMPLE: *Is she drying them?*
Yes, she is.

Reading

Use the learning strategy *Make Predictions* (see page 56).

1. Look at the pictures and the title of the story.
2. Look for words you know in the story.
3. What do you think the story is about?
4. Make a prediction.
5. Tell your prediction to your classmates.

READ THIS!

Getting Ready

Today is Saturday. Carlos and Carmen are having a party. The family is getting ready for the party. Their mother is sweeping the floor in the entranceway. Their father is vacuuming the rug. Their brother is washing the windows in the living room. Their grandmother is cooking enchiladas in the kitchen.

Their sister is washing her hair in the bathroom. She is not helping her family. Carlos and Carmen are angry.

Carlos says, "Where is Carolina? Carolina, where are you? Are you getting ready to help us?"

Carmen says, "Carolina! Car–o–lina! What are you doing? We need help! NOW!"

Mother says, "Carmen, calm down. Carolina is in the bathroom. She's getting ready for your party. She can help later."

Carmen says, "Mom, it's my party. I need time to get ready."

Carlos says, "Mom, it's my party, too. And I need time to get ready, too."

Mother says, "It's three o'clock now. The party starts at seven o'clock. You have time to get ready."

＊ ＊ ＊ ＊ ＊

It is four o'clock. Carolina is still in the bathroom. Carmen and Carlos are knocking on the door. "Carolina! Car–o–lina! What are you doing? We need the bathroom, too. It's time for us to get ready!"

Carolina says, "I can't come out."

Carmen says, "Carolina, what *are* you doing?"

Carolina is crying. "My hair is turning blue. Oh, oh, oh . . ."

"Wow!" says Carlos. "That is *very* cool! Hey, Mom! Can I have blue hair, too?"

AFTER YOU READ

A. Think about the learning strategy. What predictions did you make about the story before you read it? Were your predictions correct? As you read the story, did you need to change your predictions? What information or clues did you use to make your predictions? Discuss your answers with a classmate.

B. True or false? In your notebook, write *True* or *False* for each statement. For your *False* answers, make the sentences correct.

1. The grandmother is getting ready for the party.
2. Carmen and Carlos are excited.
3. Carolina is not helping her family.
4. Carmen is angry at Carlos.
5. Carlos and Carmen are ready for their party.

Check your work. How many of your answers are correct? Write the number of correct answers in your notebook.

Keep Trying!   Great Work!

Writing

BEFORE YOU WRITE

A. You are going to write a dialogue about two people talking on the phone. First, read the dialogue below.

> Mei: Hello, Carmen. This is Mei. What are you doing?
> Carmen: Hi, Mei. I'm studying for a test.
> Mei: What's Carlos doing?
> Carmen: He's making dinner with my mother.
> Mei: Really? What are they cooking?
> Carmen: They're cooking chili. I can smell it.
> Mei: Oh. I love chili.
> Carmen: Can you come over for dinner tonight?
> Mei: Thanks! I'll ask my mom. Bye.
> Carmen: Okay. Bye, Mei.

B. Read the *Before I Write* checklist. In your notebook, write the name of a friend, his or her questions, and your answers.

WRITE THIS!

Read the *While I Write* checklist. In your notebook, write a phone dialogue between you and a friend. Talk about what you are doing. Ask your teacher for new words.

AFTER YOU WRITE

A. Read the *After I Write* checklist. Check your work.

B. Read your dialogue with a classmate. Then help your classmate read his or her dialogue.

C. Write a final copy of your dialogue in your notebook.

Before I Write

► Study the model.

► Think about talking on the phone with a friend.

► Make notes about . . .
   who is calling me
   what my friend asks me
   how I answer my friend

While I Write

► Write the **names of the speakers** at the beginning of what they say.

> Mei: Hello, Carmen. This is Mei. What are you doing?

► Use the **present continuous** to write about what is happening now.

> What are you doing?
> I'm studying for a test.

► Use words like **he**, **she**, **they**, and **it** in place of nouns.

> They're cooking chili. I can smell it.

After I Write

► Did I write the names of the speakers at the beginning of what they say?

► Did I use the present continuous to write about what is happening now?

► Did I use words like *he, she, they,* and *it* in place of nouns?

90   **Unit 3**

Learning Log

 ## VOCABULARY

Read the words and expressions. Then copy them into your notebook.
Underline the words and expressions you need to review.

Nouns					Expressions
Places in a House		**Things in a House**		**Other**	calm down
bathroom	kitchen	bed	rug	floor	cool
bedroom	living room	door	stove	hair	get ready
entranceway		lightbulb	window	sauce	I mean . . .
					Oh, dear!
Verbs				**Adjectives**	right now
burn	help	turn		blue	
change	knock	turn off		busy	
clean	make	vacuum		later	
cook	sweep	wash			

LANGUAGE and LEARNING STRATEGIES

Copy the checklist into your notebook. Check what you know. Review what you
need to know.

I can . . .

_____ read and understand the dialogue "Help for Carlos"

_____ ask and answer questions about what I or other people are doing

_____ use object pronouns correctly

_____ read and use new words with the long vowel sounds /ā/ as in
  came, /ī/ as in *like*, /ō/ as in *close*, and /yoo/ as in *use*

_____ use the learning strategy *Make Predictions* to guess what a story
  will be about

_____ read and understand the story "Getting Ready"

_____ write a dialogue about something that is happening right now

SELF-EVALUATION QUESTIONS

Answer the questions in your notebook.

1. What is easy in Chapter 7? What is difficult in Chapter 7?

2. How can you learn the things that are difficult?

Chapter 8

I have to work.

Look at the picture. What things can you name in English? Say the words. Make sentences about what you see and what the people are doing.

A. Listen to the dialogue. Then answer this question: How many boys call Maria?

B. Read the dialogue.

The Telephone Calls

(*The telephone rings.*)

Maria: Hello?

Carlos: Hello, Maria. This is Carlos.

Maria: Hi, Carlos. It's very loud there. What are you doing?

Carlos: We're cleaning the house. Our party is tonight. Can you come?

Maria: I'm sorry, but I can't go out tonight. I have to baby-sit.

Carlos: Oh. That's too bad. Well, bye.

          ★ ★ ★ ★ ★

Mother: Who was that boy?

Maria: That was Carlos, a friend from school. He's having a party tonight, but I can't go.

Mother: Poor Maria.

          ★ ★ ★ ★ ★

(*The telephone rings.*)

Maria: Hello?

Pablo: Hi, Maria. This is Pablo.

Maria: Hi, Pablo.

Pablo: Maria, would you like to go to the party with me tonight?

Maria: Oh, Pablo, I want to go, but I can't. I have to work. I'm sorry.

Pablo: I'm sorry, too. Bye, Maria.

          ★ ★ ★ ★ ★

Mother: Who was that boy?

Maria: That was another boy in my class. Mama, I . . .

(*The telephone rings.*)

Maria: Hello?

Samir: Maria? Hi. This . . . this . . . Samir. I mean, this is Samir.

Maria:	Oh, hi, Samir.
Samir:	Umm . . . would . . . would you like to go to the party with me?
Maria:	I'm sorry, Samir, but I can't go.
Samir:	Oh. Okay. Umm . . . bye.

* * * * *

Maria:	Oh, Mama. I'm so miserable.
Mother:	Maria, go to the party. I can baby-sit for you. But you have to go with Paco.
Maria:	Oh, thank you, Mama. Thank you! I have to get ready. I'm so excited!

Pair and Group Work

A. Read the dialogue with a classmate.

B. Act out the dialogue in groups of five.

VOCABULARY

Words		Expressions
loud	another	That's too bad.
go out	miserable	Poor (Maria).
tonight	excited	Would you like to . . . ?
work		

A. Read and say the vocabulary. Then write the vocabulary in your notebook.

B. Use word analysis to study the vocabulary (see page 250, Steps 1–3).

C. Find the vocabulary in the dialogue. Then read the sentences that use the vocabulary.

D. Choose three words from the word box. In your notebook, write three questions using these words. Ask a classmate your questions. Answer your classmate's questions.

Grammar 1

Simple Present Tense and Present Continuous Tense

Simple Present	Present Continuous
I **read** every day.	I **am reading** now.
You **walk** to school every morning.	You **are walking** to school now.
Liliana **calls** her family every week.	Liliana **is calling** her family now.
Carmen and Carlos **study** every night.	Carmen and Carlos **are studying** now.

Remember: Use the simple present to tell what you usually do. Use the present continuous to tell what you are doing right now.

A. Copy the sentences into your notebook. Then fill in the blanks with the correct form of the verb.

1. Carlos and Carmen _____*are cleaning*_____ the house now.
   (clean / are cleaning)

   They _____ for their party.
   (get ready / are getting ready)

2. Pablo _____ to his grandmother on the phone now.
   (talks / is talking)

   He _____ her every Saturday.
   (calls / is calling)

3. Bic loves baseball. He _____ baseball every day after school.
   (plays / is playing)

   Right now he _____ at the park with his friends.
   (plays / is playing)

B. Read the conversation. Then listen.

   A: What are you doing?

   B: I'm watching TV.

   A: Do you watch TV every day?

   B: No, I don't.

C. Practice the conversation in Exercise B with a classmate. Then make new conversations using other phrases.

Check your Vocabulary Handbook (page 222) for other free-time activities.

Grammar 2

Statements with *like, have,* and *want* + Infinitive

Affirmative Statements			Negative Statements		
I You	like have want	to work.	I You	do not like do not have do not want	to work.
He/She	likes has wants		He/She	does not like does not have does not want	
We You They	like have want		We You They	do not like do not have do not want	

do not	=	don't
does not	=	doesn't

A. Copy the sentences into your notebook. Then fill in the blanks with the correct form of the verb. Use contractions.

1. Liliana *doesn't want* to be a lawyer. (want, negative)
2. Maria and Pablo _____ to study. (have, affirmative)
3. I _____ to go to the party. (want, affirmative)
4. Sophie _____ to make lunch. (have, negative)
5. Mr. Gomez _____ to teach English. (like, affirmative)

B. Write sentences in your notebook.

1. Write three sentences about what you have to do.
   EXAMPLE: *I have to clean my room.*
2. Write three sentences about what your friend wants to do.
   EXAMPLE: *My friend Lena wants to go to the bookstore.*
3. Write three sentences about what you and your friend like to do together.
   EXAMPLE: *My friend Julio and I like to talk on the phone.*

Word Study

Long Vowel Sound: /ā/

The letters *a_e*, *ai*, and *ay* can stand for the long vowel sound /ā/ as in *take, wait,* and *say.*

A. Use the learning strategy *Sound Out* (see page 32) and the pictures to read the words.

1. game

2. lake

3. mail

4. Spain

5. train

6. play

7. gray

8. day

B. Read the sentences aloud. Then copy them into your notebook. Circle the letters that stand for the long vowel sound /ā/.

1. Paco wants to buy a gray hat.
2. You can have lunch by the lake.
3. Do you want to play this game with me?
4. Can you mail these letters, please?
5. We have to take the six o'clock train.
6. Mr. Gomez is not from Spain.

C. Look at Exercise A. Choose two words with the long vowel sound /ā/. In your notebook, write a sentence for each word.

Grammar 3

What Questions with *like, have,* and *want* + Infinitive

What	do	I you	like have want	to do?	You I	like have want	to work.
	does	he/she	like have want	to do?	He/She	likes has wants	to work.
	do	we you they			You We They	like have want	

Copy the questions into your notebook. Then
fill in the blanks with *do* or *does*.

1. What ___*does*___ Maria like to do?
2. What _____ Bic and Pablo want to do?
3. What _____ Mei have to do?
4. What _____ he like to do?
5. What _____ you and I have to do?

Yes/No Questions with *like, have,* and *want* + Infinitive

Do	I you	like have want	to study?	Yes,	you I	do.	No,	you I	don't.
Does	he/she				he/she	does.		he/she	doesn't.
Do	we you they				you we they	do.		you we they	don't.

Write five *yes/no* questions in your notebook.
Use *like, have,* and *want* + infinitive. Then ask
a classmate your questions. Answer your
classmate's questions.

EXAMPLE: *Do you have to study tonight?*
          Yes, I do.

BEFORE YOU READ

Use the learning strategy *Use What You Know*.

1. Look at the pictures and the title of the story. Who is this story about?
2. Discuss with a classmate what you already know about this person. Do not look at the story.
3. Think about and use the learning strategy *Use What You Know* to help you read the story.

READ THIS!

Maria

Maria comes from El Salvador. She is fifteen years old. She speaks Spanish. In school, she is learning English. Now she is living in the United States. She lives with her family in an apartment.

Maria is happy most of the time. She likes Washington School. She has good friends in her class. Carmen, Mei, Liliana, Carlos, Pablo, Bic, and Samir are her best friends. Sophie is a new girl. She is also Maria's friend. Maria is very nice. The other students like her a lot.

But sometimes Maria is sad. Sometimes she feels homesick. Sometimes she wants to go back to El Salvador. She misses her friends in El Salvador. She misses her big sister in El Salvador. She misses her school in El Salvador. Everybody speaks Spanish in her school in El Salvador.

Maria is a good student, but school is hard for her. English is very hard for her. But she has to learn it. Reading is also difficult for her, but she has to learn to read, too.

At home, Maria does her homework and then she draws and paints pictures. She likes to paint and draw. She draws with pencils. She paints with pretty paints. She is very good at art, but her friends and teachers do not know this. She does not want to show her art to other people because she is very shy.

Maria works on Saturday nights. She baby-sits. Maria loves her job. She really likes children. But sometimes she wants to go out on Saturday nights.

AFTER YOU READ

A. Think about the learning strategy. What information did you know about Maria before reading? Did this information help you read? What new information did you get from this reading? Discuss your answers with a classmate.

B. Create an exercise.

1. Work with a classmate. Write five sentences about the reading in your notebook. Write three true sentences and two false sentences.

   EXAMPLE: *Maria does not like children.*

2. Exchange your sentences with another pair of students. Read their sentences. Write *True* or *False* after the sentences.

   EXAMPLE: *Maria misses El Salvador. True.*

Check your work. How many answers are correct? Write the number of correct answers in your notebook.

Keep Trying!   Great Work!

Writing

BEFORE YOU WRITE

A. You are going to write a paragraph about a classmate. First, read the paragraph below.

> Alberto is from Mexico. He is fifteen years old. He lives in the United States. Alberto likes to dance. He likes to go to the movies on weekends. He wants to be a teacher. He has to study hard.

B. Read the *Before I Write* checklist. As a class, write five to ten questions that you can ask each other. Write the questions in your notebook.

C. Use the questions you wrote in Exercise B to interview a classmate. Write your classmate's answers in your notebook.

WRITE THIS!

Read the *While I Write* checklist. Look at your notes and write a paragraph about your classmate. Ask your teacher for new words.

AFTER YOU WRITE

A. Read the *After I Write* checklist. Check your work.

B. Read your paragraph to your classmate. Check your information with your classmate. Then read your classmate's paragraph about you. Check your classmate's information.

C. Write a final copy of your paragraph in your notebook. Then make a copy and give it to your classmate.

Before I Write

▶ Study the model.

▶ Write interview questions.

▶ Interview my classmate.

▶ Make notes on my classmate's answers.

While I Write

▶ Use **he** or **she** in place of the name of a person.

> Alberto is from Mexico. He is fifteen years old.

▶ Put a **capital letter** at the beginning of the name of a country.

> He lives in the United States.

▶ Use **likes**, **has**, and **wants** + infinitive to tell about a person.

> He likes to dance.
>
> He wants to be a teacher.
>
> He has to study hard.

After I Write

▶ Did I use *he* or *she* in place of the name of a person?

▶ Did I put a capital letter at the beginning of the name of a country?

▶ Did I use *likes, has,* and *wants* + infinitive to tell about a person?

Learning Log

◆ VOCABULARY

Read the words and expressions. Then copy them into your notebook.
Underline the words and expressions you need to review.

Nouns		Adjectives		Question Word	Expressions
family	night	another	miserable	who	Poor (Maria).
home	picture	excited	most		That's too
homework		loud	shy		bad.
		homesick			Would you like
					to . . . ?
Verbs				**Adverbs**	
draw	go out	miss	show	sometimes	
feel	learn	paint	work	tonight	

◆ LANGUAGE and LEARNING STRATEGIES

Copy the checklist into your notebook. Check what you know. Review what you
need to know.

I can . . .

_____ read and understand the dialogue "The Telephone Calls"

_____ use the simple present and the present continuous correctly

_____ ask and answer questions using *like, have,* and *want* + infinitive

_____ read and use new words with the long vowel sound /ā/ as in *wait*

_____ use the learning strategy *Use What You Know* to understand
new information

_____ read and understand the story "Maria"

_____ interview a classmate and write a paragraph about him or her

◆ SELF-EVALUATION QUESTIONS

Answer the questions in your notebook.

1. What is easy in Chapter 8? What is difficult in Chapter 8?
2. How can you learn the things that are difficult?

Chapter 9

You came to our party!

Look at the picture. What things can you name in English? Say the words. Make sentences about what you see and what the people are doing.

LISTENING AND READING

A. Listen to the dialogue. Then answer this question: How old are Carmen and Carlos?

B. Read the dialogue.

Maria and Paco

Carmen: Hi, Maria. You came to our party! I'm so happy to see you.

Maria: Thanks. My mother is baby-sitting for me. She's the best. Hey . . . is it your birthday, Carmen?

Carmen: Well, . . . yes . . .

Maria: Really? How old are you? How old is Carlos?

Carmen: We're both sixteen.

Maria: Oh! So, are you . . . ah . . . what's the word in English?

Paco: Twins!

Carmen: Right! We're twins.

Maria: Oh, wow! I didn't know that. Happy birthday!

Paco: Yes, happy birthday.

Maria: Oh, I'm sorry . . . I didn't introduce you. This is Paco.

Paco: Hello. Nice to meet you.

Carmen: Hello, Paco. It's *very* nice to meet you!

＊ ＊ ＊ ＊ ＊

Carlos: Who is that guy with Maria?

Samir: I don't know. Maria said his name is Paco.

Carlos:	Why is Maria with him?
Pablo:	I don't know. I didn't talk to him. Carmen talked to him.

* * * * *

Carmen:	So, Paco, did you meet Maria at school?
Paco and Maria:	Ha! Ha! Ha!
Carmen:	What? Did I say something wrong?
Maria:	No, . . . well, . . . you said . . .
Paco:	Hey, Carmen, do you like to dance?
Carmen:	Yes, I do.
Paco:	Good! Let's dance!
Carlos, Pablo, and Samir:	Maria, let's dance!

Pair and Group Work

A. Read the dialogue with a classmate.

B. Act out the dialogue in groups of six.

VOCABULARY

Words		Expressions
come (came)	guy	I'm so happy to see you.
both	talk	(She's) the best.
twins	say (said)	Let's . . .
do (did)	something	
introduce	wrong	

A. Read and say the vocabulary. Then write the vocabulary in your notebook.

B. Use word analysis to study the vocabulary (see page 250, Steps 1–3).

C. Find the vocabulary in the dialogue. Then read the sentences that use the vocabulary.

D. Choose five of the words from the word box. In your notebook, write a mini-dialogue using these words. Practice your dialogue with a classmate.

Grammar 1

Past Tense of Regular Verbs: Affirmative Statements

Some verbs have **regular past-tense** forms.		
I You He/She We You They	**talked**	to Paco.

Add **–ed** to form the **past tense** of most regular verbs.
> EXAMPLE: *talk + ed = talked*

If a regular verb ends in **e**, just add **–d** to form the **past tense**.
> EXAMPLE: *dance + d = danced*

If a regular verb ends in a consonant + **y**, change the **y** to **i** before adding **–ed**.
> EXAMPLE: *study + i + ed = studied*

A. Write these regular verbs in your notebook. Then write the past tense forms.

1. play   _played_
2. ask   _____
3. introduce   _____
4. look   _____
5. dance   _____

6. study   _____
7. laugh   _____
8. like   _____
9. arrive   _____
10. love   _____

B. Copy the sentences into your notebook. Then fill in the blanks with the correct form of the verb.

1. I _played_ baseball after school yesterday. (play)
2. Everyone _____ the movie last night. (like)
3. You _____ to your grandmother on the phone last night. (talk)
4. I _____ my bedroom yesterday. (clean)
5. Liliana _____ on Saturday and Sunday. (study)

Grammar 2

Past Tense of Irregular Verbs: Affirmative Statements

Some verbs have **irregular past-tense** forms.		
I You He / She We You They	**came**	to the party.

come	→ came	make	→ made	
do	→ did	read	→ read	
eat	→ ate	say	→ said	
go	→ went	sing	→ sang	
have	→ had	teach	→ taught	
know	→ knew	write	→ wrote	

B. Copy the sentences into your notebook. Then fill in the blanks with the correct form of the verb.

1. Carmen _taught_ Maria some new words. (teach)
2. Maria and Paco _____ to the party. (go)
3. Mrs. Garcia _____ the math problem on the board. (write)
4. We _____ the answer to the teacher's question. (know)
5. Samir _____ two enchiladas at the party. (eat)

B. In your notebook, write three sentences about what you did yesterday. Use past tense verbs from the chart.

EXAMPLE: *I ate lunch with my friends.*

Word Study

Long Vowel Sound: /ē/

The letters *ea, ee, y, e,* and *ie* can stand for the long vowel sound /ē/ as in *me, read, meet, happy,* and *piece.* (Exceptions: *learn* and *my*)

A. Use the learning strategy *Sound Out* (see page 32) and the pictures to read the words.

1. clean   **2.** meat   **3.** tree   **4.** feet

5. baby   **6.** city   **7.** me   **8.** field

B. Read the sentences aloud. Then copy them into your notebook. Circle the letters that stand for the long vowel sound /ē/.

1. She is painting a picture of a tree.

2. I can clean my bedroom now.

3. Those shoes are too big for my feet!

4. Pablo's father needs a lightbulb.

5. We can play ball at the baseball field.

6. Sophie's aunt has a new baby.

C. Look at the dialogue on pages 102–103. Find five words with the long vowel sound /ē/. Write the words in your notebook.

Grammar 3

Past Tense: Negative Statements

Affirmative Statements			Negative Statements		
I You He/She It We You They	**arrived** **came**	late.	I You He/She It We You They	**did not arrive** **did not come**	late.
Remember: *Did* is the past tense of *do*. Use *did* to make negative statements in the past tense.					

did not = didn't

Change each statement from affirmative to negative.
Write the new sentences in your notebook. Use contractions.

1. Carlos called Pablo last night. *Carlos didn't call Pablo last night.*
2. Carmen helped her mother with the housework.
3. Liliana and Bic went to the movies yesterday.
4. Samir did his homework at the library.
5. Sophie liked her mother's new shoes.

Past Tense: *Yes/No* Questions

Did	I you he/she it we you they	**go?**	Yes,	you I he/she it you we they	**did.**	No,	you I he/she it you we they	**didn't.**
Remember: Use *did* to make *yes/no* questions in the past tense.								

Look at the sentences in the exercise above. Change each statement to a question. Write the questions in your notebook.

EXAMPLE: Carlos called Pablo last night. *Did Carlos call Pablo last night?*

Reading

Use the learning strategy *Make Inferences*.

1. Read the story.
2. When you see a new word, write it in your notebook.
3. Read the sentence that has the word. Then read the two or three sentences before and after that sentence.
4. Guess at the meaning of the new word.
5. Write or draw your guess next to the word in your notebook.

LEARNING STRATEGY

Make Inferences

When you *Make Inferences*, you use information to make good guesses about meaning.

READ THIS!

A Fun Party

Everybody at Carlos and Carmen's birthday party had fun. People laughed and talked. The music was good. People danced. The food was delicious. People ate a lot. Grandmother was happy. She danced with her grandson.

Pablo played his guitar. He sang a beautiful song. "That was wonderful, Pablo," said Mei. "I don't know that song. Is it new?"

Pablo was embarrassed. "Well," he said. "I wrote that song. Do you really like it?"

"Yes," said Mei. "Play another song, please!"

So Pablo played more songs. Then everybody danced and talked some more.

The girls talked about Paco. Who *was* Paco? No one knew. Then Carmen said, "He's very cute!"

The other girls agreed. "Yes, he is!" they said.

The boys talked about Paco, too. "Who *is* that guy Paco?" asked Carlos. No one knew.

Then Pablo said, "Maybe he's Maria's boyfriend."

The boys were not happy. "No," they said. "No way."

"I don't like him," said Carlos. The other boys agreed.

It was almost twelve o'clock. Paco said to Maria, "Maria, it's late. We have to go home."

"No," said Maria. "I'm having fun!"

"We promised Mama, Maria. Mama said, 'Come home at midnight. Don't be late!' We have to go home now."

So Maria and Paco said good-bye to everyone.

Carmen looked at her friends. She said, "I know! I know who Paco is!"

AFTER YOU READ

A. Think about the learning strategy.

1. What inferences did you make about the meanings of new words in the story? Talk about your inferences with the rest of the class.

2. At the end, Carmen says, "I know who Paco is!" Who is he? How did you make this inference?

B. Read the questions. Write the answers in your notebook. Remember to use the past tense form of the verbs.

1. What did people do at the party? *They talked, danced, and ate.*
2. Why was Grandmother happy?
3. What did Pablo do at the party?
4. What did Carmen say about Paco?
5. Why did Maria and Paco have to go home at midnight?

Check your work. How many of your answers are correct? Write the number of correct answers in your notebook.

Keep Trying!   Great Work!

Writing

A. You are going to write a letter to a friend. First, read the letter below.

> November 6, 2004 ◄—**Date**
>
> Dear Sara, ◄—**Greeting**
>
> I went to a birthday party for Carmen and Carlos on Saturday night. The party was at their house.
>
> I talked with my friends Mei and Sophie. I danced with Carlos, Pablo, and Samir. A boy named Paco came to the party with Maria.
>
> There was so much food! Carlos made enchiladas for us. I ate ice cream, too, but I didn't eat the cake.
>
> I had a lot of fun at the party. What did you do on Saturday? Please write.
>
> Your friend, ◄—**Closing**
>
> Liliana ◄—**Signature**

B. Read the *Before I Write* checklist. In your notebook, make notes about a party or event you went to.

WRITE THIS!

Read the *While I Write* checklist. Look at your notes and write a letter to a friend about the party or event you went to. Ask your teacher for new words.

AFTER YOU WRITE

A. Read the *After I Write* checklist. Check your work.

B. Read your letter to a classmate. Then listen to your classmate read his or her letter.

C. Write a final copy of your letter in your notebook.

Tools for Writing

Before I Write

▶ Study the model.

▶ Think about a party or an event.

▶ Make notes about . . .

where the party or event was
who came to the party or event
what I did at the party or event
what my friends did at the party or event

While I Write

▶ Write the **date** in the upper right-hand corner of my letter.

November 6, 2004

▶ Put a comma at the end of the **greeting** and the **closing**.

Dear Sara,

Your friend,

▶ Use words like **went, talked,** and **came** to write about the past.

I went to a birthday party.

After I Write

▶ Did I write the date in the upper right-hand corner of my letter?

▶ Did I put a comma at the end of the greeting and the closing?

▶ Did I use words like *went, talked,* and *came* to write about the past?

Learning Log

◆ VOCABULARY

Read the words and expressions. Then copy them into your notebook.
Underline the words and expressions you need to review.

Nouns		Adjectives		Question Word	Expressions
People	**Other**	beautiful	embarrassed	why	I'm so happy to
boyfriend	guitar	both	wonderful		see you.
everybody	midnight	cute	wrong		Let's . . .
grandson	something	delicious			No way.
guy	song				(She's) the
twins					best.

Verbs		
agree	introduce	say (said)
come (came)	know (knew)	sing (sang)
do (did)	laugh	talk
eat (ate)	play	write (wrote)
have (had)	promise	

◆ LANGUAGE and LEARNING STRATEGIES

Copy the checklist into your notebook. Check what you know. Review what you
need to know.

I can . . .

_____ read and understand the dialogue "Maria and Paco"

_____ ask and answer questions using the past tense

_____ read and use new words with the long vowel sound /ē/ as in *me*

_____ use the learning strategy *Make Inferences* to learn new words

_____ read and understand the story "A Fun Party"

_____ write a letter about a party or event I went to

◆ SELF-EVALUATION QUESTIONS

Answer the questions in your notebook.

1. What is easy in Chapter 9? What is difficult in Chapter 9?
2. How can you learn the things that are difficult?

UNIT 4

AROUND TOWN

Chapter 10

How much is it?

GETTING READY

Look at the picture. What things can you name in English? Say the words. Make sentences about what you see and what the people are doing.

LISTENING AND READING

A. Listen to the dialogue. Then answer this question: Does Pablo have a new job?

B. Read the dialogue.

Pablo's New Clothes

Pablo: Carlos, can you help me find some new clothes? I need a shirt and a pair of pants.

Carlos: Sure, Pablo. Why do you need new clothes?

Pablo: Well, umm . . . It's a secret.

Carlos: Do you have a new job?

Pablo: No, not exactly.

Carlos: Okay, then, who's the lucky girl?

Pablo: What do you mean?

Carlos: Do you have a new girlfriend?

Pablo: No! Don't ask so many questions.

* * * * *

Salesclerk: Excuse me. May I help you?

Pablo: Yes. Where are the shirts?

Salesclerk: Right over there.

Pablo: Thank you.

Salesclerk: You're welcome.

* * * * *

Carlos: There are a lot of shirts here. What color do you want?

Pablo: I want a dark color.

Carlos: Here's one. It's dark blue.

Pablo: Cool! How much is it?

Carlos: It's not expensive . . . it's $15.95. Hey! Look at these cool jeans!

Pablo: No way! I don't need casual pants. I need something formal . . . you know, dress pants.

Carlos:	Oh, okay.
Pablo:	I like this dark blue pair. It matches the shirt.
Carlos:	Yeah. They look good together.
Pablo:	I need to try on the pants. But you don't have to wait. Meet me at the fountain at six o'clock.
Carlos:	Meet you at the fountain? But, Pablo, wait. . . .

Pair and Group Work

A. Read the dialogue with a classmate.

B. Act out the dialogue in groups of three.

VOCABULARY

Words		Expressions
clothes	dark	not exactly
shirt	expensive	What do you mean?
a pair of	jeans	May I help you?
pants	casual	right over there
secret	formal	You're welcome.
lucky	dress pants	
girlfriend	try on	

A. Read and say the vocabulary. Then write the vocabulary in your notebook.

B. Use word analysis to study the vocabulary (see pages 250–251, Steps 1–3).

C. Find the vocabulary in the dialogue. Read the sentences that use the vocabulary.

D. Work with a classmate. Choose a word from the word box and draw a picture of it. Don't speak. Your classmate has to guess which word you are drawing. Take turns.

Grammar 1

Information Questions with *be*: Present Tense

Who is that boy?	He is my brother.
What are their names?	Their names are Chi Chen and Chi Wan.
When is the school dance?	It is on Saturday.
Where is the library?	It is next to the gym.
Why are you sad?	I am sad because I cannot go to the dance.
How is your sister?	She is fine.

who is	=	who's
what is	=	what's
where is	=	where's
how is	=	how's

Read each answer. Then write the question it responds to in your notebook.

1. <u>Her name</u> is Akiko. (What)
   What is her name?
2. <u>She is happy</u> because it is your birthday. (Why)
3. <u>The party</u> is at her house. (Where)
4. Her friend Kelly <u>made the cake</u>. (Who)
5. <u>Akiko is feeling</u> very happy. (How)

Information Questions with *be*: Past Tense

To ask about something in the past, use a past-tense form of *be*:

    EXAMPLES: **When was** the party?
                Where were you yesterday?

Copy the questions into your notebook. Then fill in the blanks with the correct question words and the correct form of *be*.

1. ___*How*___ ___*was*___ the movie last night? It was great!
2. _____ _____ you late for class? Because I had to go to the office.
3. _____ _____ the party? It was at Pat's house.
4. _____ _____ the test? It was last Monday.
5. _____ _____ your first teacher's name? Her name was Ms. Shay.

Grammar 2

Information Questions with *do*: Present Tense

Who does Maria want to call?	She wants to call her sister.
What does he need?	He needs a shirt and some shoes.
When do you go shopping?	I go shopping on Saturdays.
Where do they go after school?	They go home after school.
Why does she look sad?	She looks sad because she is lost.
How does this shirt look?	It looks nice.

Read each answer. Then write the question it responds to in your notebook.

1. He comes from Lebanon. (Where) *Where does he come from?*
2. Mr. Gomez's students study English. (What)
3. We get to school at seven-thirty. (When)
4. I see my friend Amelia. (Who)
5. His shoes look cool. (How)

Information Questions with *do*: Past Tense

To ask about something in the past, use a past-tense form of *do*:

EXAMPLES: **When did** you eat dinner?
            Why did she go to the library?

Write a dialogue about your dinner last night in your notebook. Complete the questions and write true answers. Then practice the dialogue with a classmate.

A: When *did you eat dinner*?   B: *I ate dinner at seven*.

A: Where _____?   B: _____.

A: Who _____?   B: _____.

A: What _____?   B: _____.

Word Study

Long Vowel Sound: /ī/

The letters *i, y, i_e, ie,* and *igh* can stand for the long vowel sound /ī/ as in *hi, my, time, pie,* and *right.*

A. Use the learning strategy *Sound Out* (see page 32) and the pictures to read the words.

1. child

2. cry

3. dime

4. size

5. pie

6. tie

7. right

8. night

B. Read the sentences. Then copy them into your notebook. Circle the letters that stand for the long vowel sound /ī/.

1. Are you baking a pie?

2. Turn right at the gym.

3. Why does he need a new tie?

4. I need a dime.

5. What size dress does she wear?

6. We can go to the movies on Friday night.

C. Look at the dialogue on pages 114–115. Find four words with the long vowel sound /ī/. Write the words in your notebook.

Grammar 3

Questions with *how much*

How much	is	this that?	
	are	these those?	

How much	does	this that	cost?
	do	these those	

A. Copy the questions into your notebook. Then fill in the blanks with the correct form of the verb.

1. How much ___*is*___ that book?
   (is / are)

2. How much _____ this jacket cost?
   (do / does)

3. How much _____ those brown pants?
   (is / are)

4. How much _____ this shirt?
   (is / are)

5. How much _____ these shoes cost?
   (do / does)

B. Read the conversation. Then listen.

A: How much does this shirt cost?
B: It's $13.99.
A: And how much are those jeans?
B: They're $25.99.

C. Practice the conversation in Exercise B with a classmate. Then make new conversations using your own information.

Check your Vocabulary Handbook (page 225) for other clothes.

Reading

BEFORE YOU READ

Use the learning strategy *Make Predictions* (see page 56).

1. Look at the pictures and the title of the story.
2. Look for words you know in the story.
3. What do you think the story is about?
4. Make a prediction.
5. Tell your prediction to your classmates.

READ THIS!

A Forty-Dollar Dress

Maria wanted a new dress. Carmen and Mei went shopping with her. They went to a department store in town.

Carmen showed a nice dress to Maria. "What do you think?" she asked Maria.

"Oh, yes," said Maria. "I like it. How much is it?"

Carmen read the price tag. "Wow!" she said. "It costs a hundred and fifty dollars!"

"Forget it," said Maria. "I only have forty dollars."

Mei showed Maria a sweater and skirt. Maria did not like the sweater and skirt. But she said, "They're . . . umm . . . nice. How much are they?"

Mei read the price tags. The sweater and skirt together cost fifty dollars.

Maria said, "These are very nice, Mei. But I only have forty dollars. And I want a dress."

The girls looked at more dresses. Maria found something. She showed it to Carmen and Mei. "I love this one!" she said. "And it costs forty dollars!"

Mei said, "Maria, that isn't a good color for you!"

Carmen agreed with Mei. "You know, Maria, Mei's right. It's not a good color for you."

Suddenly, Mei said, "Oh, no! It's ten minutes to three. I have to be at the supermarket at three o'clock."

"Why do you have to be at the supermarket at three o'clock?" asked Maria.

Mei answered, "I'm meeting my sister, Amy, there. We have to buy some things for our grandmother. Come with me."

Maria said, "Okay, but I have to be at the fountain at six o'clock."

Carmen looked at Mei. Then she looked at Maria. "Why do you have to be at the fountain at six o'clock?" she asked.

"I have to meet Pablo," answered Maria.

Carmen said, "Pablo?"

"Yes," said Maria. "At six o'clock."

Both Carmen and Mei said, "We do, too!"

AFTER YOU READ

A. Think about the learning strategy. What predictions did you make about the story before you read it? Were your predictions correct? As you read the story, did you need to change your predictions? What information or clues did you use to make your predictions?

B. Read the questions. Then write the answers in your notebook.

1. Who went shopping with Maria?
2. Why didn't Maria buy the first dress?
3. Why didn't Mei and Carmen like the forty-dollar dress?
4. Why does Mei have to go to the supermarket?
5. Where do the girls have to be at six o'clock?

Check your work. How many of your answers are correct? Write the number of correct answers in your notebook.

Writing

BEFORE YOU WRITE

A. You are going to write a script for a fashion show. First, read the script below.

Carmen:	Good afternoon. Welcome to our fashion show. Here comes Liliana Cruz. What are you wearing, Liliana?
Liliana:	I'm wearing a red dress and a black cape.
Carmen:	Thank you, Liliana. You look great! Now, everyone, who's that? He has his back turned. He's dressed in white pants and a jacket. Wait! He's turning around. It's Samir! He's holding a black guitar. Wow! Samir, how much does that suit cost?
Samir:	Only fifty dollars—without the guitar.
Carmen:	Thank you, Samir.

B. Read the *Before I Write* checklist. In your notebook, make notes about the people and the clothes in a school fashion show.

WRITE THIS!

Read the *While I Write* checklist. Look at your notes and write a script for a school fashion show. Ask your teacher for new words.

AFTER YOU WRITE

A. Read the *After I Write* checklist. Then check your work.

B. Read your script to a classmate. Then listen to your classmate read his or her script.

C. Write a final copy of your script in your notebook.

Before I Write

▶ Study the model.

▶ Think about a school fashion show.

▶ Make notes about . . .
  what the people wear
  what the people say and do

While I Write

▶ Use contractions like **who's** and **it's** when speaking informally.

  Who's that?
  It's Samir.

▶ Use **adjectives** to talk about the clothes.

  I'm wearing a red dress and a black cape.

▶ Ask **information questions**.

  What are you wearing?

After I Write

▶ Did I use contractions like *who's* and *it's* when speaking informally?

▶ Did I use adjectives to talk about the clothes?

▶ Did I ask information questions?

Learning Log

◆ VOCABULARY

Read the words and expressions. Then copy them into your notebook. Underline the words and expressions you need to review.

Nouns				Expressions
Clothing		**Other**		Forget it.
clothes	pants	a pair of	girlfriend	May I help you?
dress	shirt	color	price tag	not exactly
dress pants	skirt	department store	secret	right over there
jeans	sweater	fountain	supermarket	What do you mean?
				You're welcome.

Verbs		Adjectives		Adverb
buy	shop	casual	formal	suddenly
cost	try on	dark	lucky	
find (found)		expensive	only	

◆ LANGUAGE and LEARNING STRATEGIES

Copy the checklist into your notebook. Check what you know. Review what you need to know.

I can . . .

_____ read and understand the dialogue "Pablo's New Clothes"

_____ ask and answer information questions with *be* and *do*

_____ read and use new words with the long vowel sound /ī/ as in *my*

_____ use the learning strategy *Make Predictions* to guess what a story will be about

_____ read and understand the story "A Forty-Dollar Dress"

_____ write a script describing what people are wearing

◆ SELF-EVALUATION QUESTIONS

Answer the questions in your notebook.

1. What is easy in Chapter 10? What is difficult in Chapter 10?
2. How can you learn the things that are difficult?

Chapter 11

She needs some lettuce.

Look at the picture. What words would you like to know? Draw pictures of them in your notebook. When you learn the words, write them next to your pictures.

A. Listen to the dialogue. Then answer this question: Does Mei's grandmother need any broccoli?

B. Read the dialogue.

I'm *So* Hungry!

Maria: Okay, so far we have potatoes and carrots. Does your grandmother need any broccoli, Amy?

Amy: Let's see . . . she needs some lettuce, but she doesn't need any broccoli.

Carmen: Wow. Looking at all this food makes me hungry. What else do we have to get?

Maria: Let's see . . . umm . . . a gallon of milk and a dozen eggs.

Carmen: Okay. I can get the milk. Maria, why don't you get the eggs?

Maria: Sure.

Mei: Did you get the lettuce, Maria?

Maria: Yes, I did.

Carmen: Can we get something to eat now? I'm *so* hungry!

Maria: Oh, Carmen, let's help Mei and Amy. Then we can get something to eat.

Mei: We're almost finished, Carmen. Hang in there.

Amy: I have some crackers in my bag . . .

Carmen: Good! Because I'm . . .

Mei and Maria: *SO* HUNGRY!

★ ★ ★ ★ ★

Cashier: The total is $57.04.

Amy: Here you are.

Cashier: Thank you. Here's your receipt.

Mei: Let's see, we have to meet Pablo at the fountain at six o'clock, so we have time to eat something. Let's go to Ricky's.

Maria: Good idea. I'm hungry!

Carmen: Not me. I'm not hungry anymore.

Girls: Ha! Ha! Ha!

Pair and Group Work

A. Read the dialogue with a classmate.

B. Act out the dialogue in groups of five.

VOCABULARY

Words			Expressions
potato	get	cracker	so far
carrot	gallon	total	Let's see . . .
broccoli	milk	receipt	Why don't you . . . ?
lettuce	dozen	anymore	Hang in there.
hungry	egg		Here you are.
else	finished		Good idea.

A. Read and say the vocabulary. Then write the vocabulary in your notebook.

B. Use word analysis to study the vocabulary (see pages 250–251, Steps 1–3).

C. Find the vocabulary in the dialogue. Read the sentences that use the vocabulary.

D. Choose five words from the word box. In your notebook, write five sentences using these words.

Word Study

Long Vowel Sound: /ō/

The letters o, oe, o_e, oa, and ow can stand for the long vowel sound /ō/ as in go, Joe, those, coat, and know.

A. Use the learning strategy *Sound Out* (see page 32) and the pictures to read the words.

1. cold   **2.** toe   **3.** hose   **4.** stove

5. toast   **6.** oak   **7.** yellow   **8.** window

B. Read the sentences. Then copy them into your notebook. Circle the letters that stand for the long vowel sound /ō/.

1. It's so cold today.

2. Can you please close the window?

3. Paco is sitting under the oak.

4. David is making some toast.

5. Where is the hose?

6. Liliana wants a yellow sweater.

C. Look at the dialogue on pages 124–125. Find four words with the long vowel sound /ō/. Write the words in your notebook.

Grammar 3

Conjunctions: *and*, *but*, and *so*

Mei is hungry,	**and** Sophie is hungry, too.
	but Carmen isn't hungry.
	so she's eating some cookies.

Remember: Use *and* to show that two ideas are similar. Use *but* to show that two ideas are different. Use *so* to show why one idea comes from another idea.

A. Copy the sentences into your notebook. Then fill in the blanks with *and, but,* or *so*.

1. Mei wanted a glass of lemonade, ___*and*___ Sophie wanted some lemonade, too.
2. Mei's grandmother needed some lettuce, _____ she didn't need any broccoli.
3. Carmen ate some crackers, _____ she wasn't hungry anymore.
4. Carmen didn't want any cookies, _____ she wanted some lemonade.
5. Mei and Sophie were hungry, _____ they had some cookies.

B. Read the conversation. Then listen.

A: I'm going to the store. What do we need?

B: We need milk, and we need bread.

A: Do we have any fruit?

B: We have some apples, but we don't have any bananas.

C. Practice the conversation in Exercise B with a classmate. Then make new conversations using your own information.

Check your Vocabulary Handbook (page 226) for other foods.

Reading

As you read, use the learning strategy *Use Selective Attention* (see page 66) to answer this question: Who works at Ricky's?

READ THIS!

At Ricky's

Mei, Maria, and Carmen went to Ricky's to get something to eat.

They waited in line. Mei looked at the cashier behind the counter, and then she asked Carmen, "Is that Paco?"

Carmen looked. Then she said, "Look, Maria! It's your brother!"

"Yes, I know," said Maria. "Paco works here."

Paco said hello to Maria and the other two girls. Then he asked them, "What do you want to eat?"

Maria said, "I want a hamburger, some French fries, and a soda." Mei ordered a salad and a cup of water. Paco asked her, "Do you want any French fries?"

Mei wanted some French fries, but she did not have enough money.

"It's okay, Mei," said Maria. "You can share my fries."

Then Paco asked Carmen, "What can I get for you?"

Carmen said, "Oh, I don't know. What's good here, Paco?"

Paco thought for a moment. Then he said, "Everything is good here."

"Oh," said Carmen. "I can't decide. What do *you* think, Paco?"

"I don't know," said Paco. "But . . . but . . . Carmen . . ."

"Yes, Paco . . ."

"Carmen, there *are* other customers behind you," said Paco.

"Come on, Carmen," said Maria. "What do you want?"

"Oh, a cup of water," said Carmen. "I'm just not hungry."

The other girls laughed. "Carmen, you're so silly!" said Maria.

Then Carlos, Bic, and Samir came in. They sat with the girls.

"Hurry up," said Carlos to the others. "It's almost six o'clock. We have to go to the fountain."

AFTER YOU READ

A. Did you use the learning strategy *Use Selective Attention* to find the answer to the question in *Before You Read*? Find the sentences in the story that answer the question. Discuss your answers with a classmate.

B. Work in groups of five or more to act out the story. Look at the story again. Read the words in quotation marks to act out the story.

C. Write the answer to these questions in your notebook.

1. What's Paco's job title?
2. What did Maria order at Ricky's?
3. Why didn't Mei order any French fries?
4. Why didn't Carmen order any food?

Check your work. How many of your answers are correct? Write the number of correct answers in your notebook.

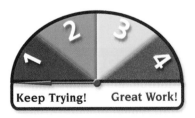

Keep Trying!   Great Work!

Chapter 12

He's the cutest guy at school.

Look at the picture. What words do you know? Say the words. Make sentences about what you see and what the people are doing.

A. Listen to the dialogue. Then answer this question: How much money does Sophie want to borrow?

B. Read the dialogue.

I Love R&B!

Sophie: Look, Liliana. This is my favorite CD store. Do we have time to stop here?

Liliana: I think so. It's only a quarter to six.

Sophie: Good. This store has the best R&B music section.

Liliana: Really? I love R&B!

Sophie: So do I. It's cooler than rock. Everybody thinks so.

Liliana: Well, not everybody. Maria says Paco likes rock music.

Sophie: *Paco!* He's the cutest guy at school. It's too bad he's older than we are.

Liliana: Do you like Paco?

Sophie: Well, he's nice, but I don't *like* Paco. I mean . . . I like guys my own age.

Liliana: Oh . . . I don't think Paco is very old. Maybe just one or two years older than we are.

Sophie: Still, I like younger guys . . . hey! Do *you* like Paco?

Liliana: He *is* cute . . . but . . .

Sophie: Well, anyway . . . let's go in.

* * * * *

Sophie: Look! Beyoncé! I love this CD. I want to buy it.

Liliana: But it's expensive, Sophie.

Sophie:	I know. But I really want this one. It's her best CD.
Liliana:	And it's her most expensive one. Do you have enough money?
Sophie:	Actually, no, I don't. Can I borrow three dollars?
Liliana:	I'm not sure I have enough money. I want to buy this CD, "20 Greatest Rock Hits."
Sophie:	A *rock* CD?
Liliana:	I'm just kidding. I'm not buying this. Here you are . . . three dollars.
Sophie:	Thanks, Liliana! You're my very best friend!

Pair Work

Read the dialogue with a classmate.

VOCABULARY

Words		Expressions
section	younger	have time
older	anyway	I think so.
own	actually	So do I.
age		I'm just kidding.

A. Read and say the vocabulary. Then write the vocabulary in your notebook.

B. Use word analysis to study the vocabulary (see pages 250–251, Steps 1–3).

C. Find the vocabulary in the dialogue. Read the sentences that use the vocabulary.

D. Choose five words from the word box. In your notebook, write five sentences using these words.

Grammar 1

Comparative Adjectives

> **Comparative adjectives** compare two people or things.
> EXAMPLES: Sophie **is taller than** Mei.
> Mei **is shorter than** Sophie.

> Add **–er** to form the comparative of most short adjectives.
> EXAMPLE: tall + er = taller
> If an adjective ends in **e**, just add **–r** to make it comparative.
> EXAMPLE: nice + r = nicer
> If an adjective ends in a consonant + **y**, change the **y** to **i** before adding **–er**.
> EXAMPLE: pretty + i + er = prettier

A. Copy the words into your notebook. Then write the comparative forms.

1. long _longer_   **4.** late _____

2. easy _____   **5.** early _____

3. hard _____   **6.** funny _____

B. Copy the sentences into your notebook. Then fill in the blanks with the correct form of the adjective.

1. Sam is _younger_ than Luis. (young)

2. Luis is _____ than Sam. (old)

3. Sam is _____ than Luis. (short)

▲ Luis   ▲ Sam

4. The cat is _____ than the dog. (small)

5. The dog is _____ than the cat. (large)

6. The cat is _____ than the dog. (cute)

Grammar 2

Superlative Adjectives

> **Superlative adjectives** compare three or more people or things.
> EXAMPLES: Pablo is the **tallest** boy.
> Bic is the **shortest** boy.

> Add **–est** to form the superlative of most short adjectives.
> EXAMPLE: *tall + est = tallest*
>
> If an adjective ends in **e**, just add **–st** to make it superlative.
> EXAMPLE: *nice + st = nicest*
>
> If an adjective ends in a consonant + **y**, change the **y** to **i** before adding **–est**.
> EXAMPLE: *pretty + i + est = prettiest*

A. Copy the words into your notebook. Then write the superlative forms.

1. easy _easiest_
2. hard _____
3. young _____
4. old _____
5. large _____
6. dirty _____

B. Copy the sentences into your notebook. Then fill in the blanks with the correct form of the adjective.

1. Yolanda's hair is the _longest_. (longer, longest)
2. Betty's hair is the _____. (shorter, shortest)
3. Trish's hair is _____ than Betty's hair. (longer, longest)

▲ Yolanda   ▲ Trish   ▲ Betty

▲ Yolanda   ▲ Trish   ▲ Betty

4. Yolanda's hat is the _____. (funnier, funniest)
5. Trish's hat is _____ than Betty's hat. (prettier, prettiest)
6. Betty's hat is _____ than Yolanda's hat. (smaller, smallest)

Reading

Use the learning strategy *Use What You Know* (see page 98).

1. Look at the pictures and the title of the story. Who is this story about?
2. Discuss with a classmate what you already know about this person. Do not look at the story.
3. Think about and use the learning strategy *Use What You Know* to help you read the story.

READ THIS!

Pablo's Surprise

The friends arrived at the fountain at ten minutes after six o'clock. They saw a stage and a lot of people in front of the fountain.

"We're a little late," said Mei. "Where's Pablo?"

"Shh," said Carlos. "The man on the stage is talking."

The man on the stage said, "Ladies and gentlemen, thank you for coming to our show. First, we have a young performer from Hillside School, Sally Miller. Please welcome Sally!"

Everyone clapped their hands. Someone yelled, "Go, Sally!"

The performer came onto the stage. She looked nervous. She told a funny story. Everyone laughed at the story, but the storyteller still looked nervous.

After the storyteller finished, the man said, "Ladies and gentlemen, next we have a young singer from Washington School. Please welcome Pablo Sanchez!"

Everyone clapped their hands. Carlos and Bic yelled, "Go, Pablo!"

Pablo walked onto the stage. He had his guitar.

"Wow!" said Carmen. "So *this* is Pablo's big secret!"

"Good evening," said Pablo. And then he started to sing a funny song. Everyone liked the song and laughed and clapped.

Maria said, "Pablo is a lot funnier than that girl was!" Her friends agreed.

Then Pablo sang a love song about a beautiful girl. Each girl thought, "Is he singing that song about me?"

After the love song, Pablo said, "And now I have a poem. The author of this poem is Jorge Luján. He's from Argentina."

> *In the darkness*
> *hundreds of cats and their kittens*
> *blink their eyes.*
> *Or are they fireflies?*

The audience clapped. Everyone liked Pablo's songs and the poem. Sophie said, "I think Pablo's second song was the prettiest."

After the show, Pablo's friends were excited. "Good job, Pablo!" said Samir.

"You were great," said Carlos.

"Yes," said Carmen. "But can we get something to eat now? I only had a cup of water for dinner, and now I'm . . ."

"*SO* HUNGRY!" said her friends, laughing.

AFTER YOU READ

A. Think about the learning strategy. What information did you know about Pablo before reading? Did this information help you read? What new information did you get from this reading? Discuss your answers with a classmate.

B. True or false? In your notebook, write *True* or *False* for each statement. For your *False* answers, make the sentences correct.

1. Pablo's friends were on time for the show.
2. Pablo sang two songs and read one poem.
3. The performer before Pablo, Sally Miller, told a funny story.
4. Pablo's friends thought Sally Miller's story was funnier than Pablo's song.
5. Sophie thought Pablo's first song was the prettiest.

Keep Trying!   Great Work!

Check your work. How many of your answers are correct? Write the number of correct answers in your notebook.

Writing

A. You are going to write words for a song. First, read the words of the song below.

The sun shines brightest
Wherever you are.
The breeze blows lightest
Wherever you are.
So remember, my love,
Never travel too far.
For I can only be happy
Wherever you are.

B. Read the *Before I Write* checklist. In your notebook, write about a strong feeling.

WRITE THIS!

Read the *While I Write* checklist. In your notebook, write words for a song. Ask your teacher for new words.

AFTER YOU WRITE

A. Read the *After I Write* checklist. Then check your work.

B. Read your song to a classmate. Then listen to your classmate read his or her song.

C. Write a final copy of your song in your notebook.

Tools for Writing

Before I Write

▶ Study the model.

▶ Think about the feeling the words express.

▶ Make notes about . . .

  a strong feeling I have had
  words that express my feeling

While I Write

▶ Use words with *-er* and *-est* to make comparisons.

  The sun shines brightest

▶ Use **rhyme** and **repetition** to give a musical feeling.

  The sun shines brightest
  Wherever you are.
  The breeze blows lightest
  Wherever you are.

▶ Use words that tell how I feel.

  For I can only be happy
  Wherever you are.

After I Write

▶ Did I use words with *-er* and *-est* to make comparisons?

▶ Did I use rhyme and repetition to give a musical feeling?

▶ Did I use words that tell how I feel?

Learning Log

◆ VOCABULARY

Read the words and expressions. Then copy them into your notebook.
Underline the words and expressions you need to review.

Nouns					Expressions
People		*Other*			Good job.
audience	performer	age	hand	section	have time
author	singer	darkness	kitten	stage	I think so.
people	storyteller	fireflies	poem		I'm just kidding.
					So do I.

Verbs		Adjectives		Adverbs
blink	yell	older	younger	actually
clap		own		anyway

◆ LANGUAGE and LEARNING STRATEGIES

Copy the checklist into your notebook. Check what you know. Review what you
need to know.

I can . . .

_____ read and understand the dialogue "I Love R&B!"

_____ compare two or three people or things

_____ read and use new words with the long vowel sound /yoo/ as in *unit*

_____ use the learning strategy *Use What You Know* to understand new
information

_____ read and understand the story "Pablo's Surprise"

_____ write words for a song

◆ SELF-EVALUATION QUESTIONS

Answer the questions in your notebook.

1. What is easy in Chapter 12? What is difficult in Chapter 12?
2. How can you learn the things that are difficult?

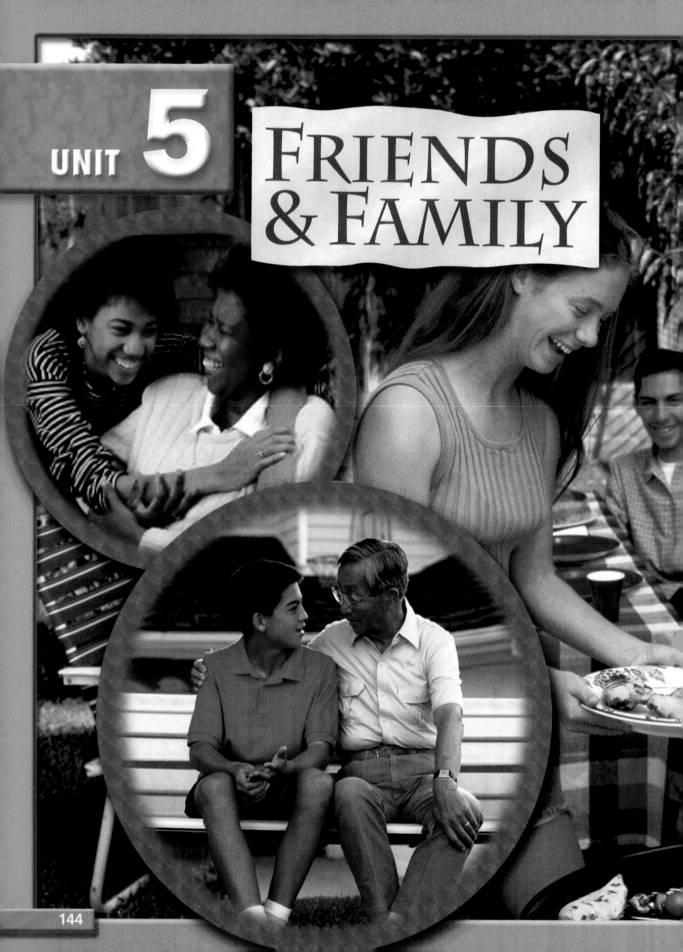

UNIT **5**

FRIENDS & FAMILY

GOALS

In Unit 5 you will learn to . . .

- listen to and read dialogues and stories about students interacting with their friends and family

- ask and answer questions about future plans

- give commands

- study words with other vowel sounds

- write about your weekend plans, something that happened to you, and a personal goal

- use the learning strategies *Make Inferences*, *Use Selective Attention*, and *Personalize*

He's going to fall!

GETTING READY

Look at the picture. What things can you name in English? Say the words. Talk about what is happening in the picture.

LISTENING AND READING

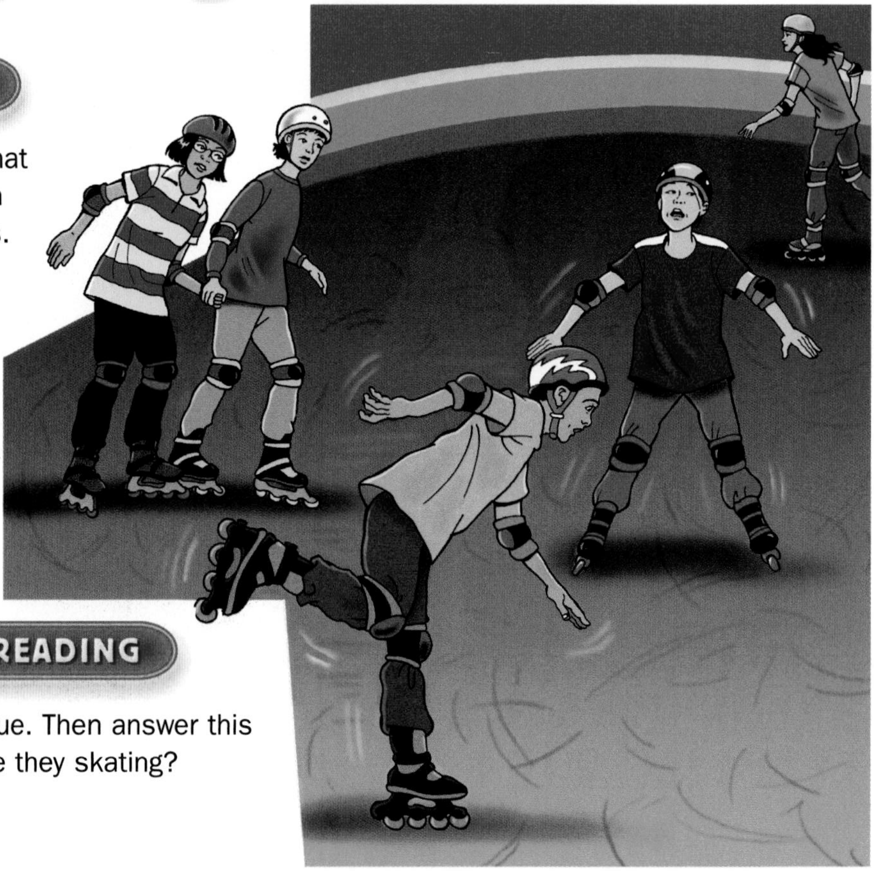

A. Listen to the dialogue. Then answer this question: Where are they skating?

B. Read the dialogue.

The Accident

Carlos: Look at me! I can skate on one foot . . .

Carmen: Be careful, Carlos! You're going to fall and break your leg!

Carlos: Don't worry, Carmen. I know what I'm doing.

Bic: Hey! Look over there at Maria! She skates really well.

Carlos: Yeah, she does.

Liliana: See you later. I want to go and ask Maria something.

Carmen: What are you going to ask her?

Liliana: I'm going to ask her to give me some skating lessons!

Carmen: That sounds like a good idea! I want to go with you.

Bic: Me, too!

Carlos: Yeah! Come on, Bic. Let's race!

Carmen: Be careful.

* * * * *

Liliana: Oh, no! Carlos is skating too fast. He's going to fall.

Carmen: Oh, no! He *did* fall!

* * * * *

Carlos: Ouch! I hurt my arm. And my leg
          hurts, too.
Carmen: Don't move, Carlos. Be still!
Liliana: What are we going to do?
Carmen: I'm going to call 911.
Liliana: Here, Carmen! Use my cell phone.
Carmen: Hello? We have an emergency. My
          brother fell down. We think he
          broke his arm and his leg. We're at
          Jackson Park . . . Yes, on State
          Street . . . Thank you! And please hurry!

 **Pair and Group Work**

A. Read the dialogue with a classmate.

B. Act out the dialogue in groups of four.

VOCABULARY

Words		Expressions
skate	race	Be careful.
foot	fast	See you later.
fall (fell)	hurt	That sounds like . . .
break (broke)	arm	Ouch!
leg	emergency	
lesson		

A. Read and say the vocabulary. Then write the vocabulary in your notebook.

B. Use word analysis to study the vocabulary (see pages 250–251, Steps 1–3).

C. Find the vocabulary in the dialogue. Read the sentences that use
the vocabulary.

D. Work with a classmate. Choose a word from the word box and draw a picture
of it. Don't speak. Your classmate has to guess which word you are drawing.
Take turns.

Grammar 1

Future Tense with *be going to*: Statements

Affirmative Statements					Negative Statements				
I	am				I	am not			
You	are				You	are not			
He/She	is	**going to**	fall.		He/She	is not	**going to**	fall.	
We					We				
You	are				You	are not			
They					They				

is not	=	isn't
are not	=	aren't

Copy the sentences into your notebook. Then fill in the blanks
with the correct form of *be going to* future. Use contractions in the negative answers.

1. Carlos <u>*is going to*</u> go to the hospital. (affirmative)
2. Carmen _____ call her parents. (affirmative)
3. Carlos's parents _____ be happy. (negative)
4. Liliana and Bic _____ go home. (affirmative)
5. Carlos _____ be at school for a while. (negative)

Future Tense with *be going to*: Yes/No Questions

Am	I				you	are.		you	aren't.
Are	you				I	am.		I'm not.	
Is	he/she	**going to**	fall?	Yes,	he/she	is.	No,	he/she	isn't.
	we				you			you	
Are	you				we	are.		we	aren't.
	they				they			they	

Read each answer. Write the question it responds to in your notebook.

1. I'm going to watch TV tonight. *Are you going to watch TV tonight?*
2. The teacher is going to be at school tomorrow.
3. I'm going to do homework after school.
4. My family is going to go to the movies this weekend.
5. I'm going to clean my room this weekend.

Grammar 2

Future Tense with *be going to*: Information Questions

What is Mei **going to** do?	She's going to buy a gift.
Who is she **going to** buy it for?	She's going to buy it for her grandmother.
When is she **going to** buy it?	She's going to buy it on Saturday.
Where is she **going to** buy it?	She's going to buy it at the department store.

A. Write the numbers 1–4 in your notebook. Read the dialogue below. Then write a question for each answer.

    A: **(1)** _What are you going to do this weekend?_ (What/do this weekend?)

    B: I'm going to go to the movies.

    A: **(2)** _____? (When/go?)

    B: I'm going to go Saturday night.

    A: **(3)** _____? (What/see?)

    B: I'm going to see *New York Story*.

    A: **(4)** _____? (Where/see?)

    B: I'm going to see it at the Metro Theater.

B. Read the conversation. Then listen.

    A: What are you going to do this weekend?

    B: I'm going to play soccer.

    A: Where are you going to play?

    B: I'm going to play in the park.

    A: Who are you going to play with?

    B: I'm going to play with my friends.

C. Practice the conversation in Exercise B with a classmate. Then make new conversations with your own information. Talk about this weekend or tonight.

Check your Vocabulary Handbook (page 222) for other activities.

Word Study

Other Vowel Sound: /o͞o/

The letters *oo*, *u_e*, *ue*, and *ew* can stand for the vowel sound /o͞o/ as in *school*, *rule*, *true*, and *new*.

A. Use the learning strategy *Sound Out* (see page 32) and the pictures to read the words.

1. food

2. moon

3. shampoo

4. June

5. glue

6. blue

7. flew

8. drew

B. Read the sentences aloud. Then copy them into your notebook. Circle the letters that stand for the vowel sound /o͞o/.

1. In June, Pablo is going to go fishing with his dad.

2. The birds flew over the house.

3. Does Anita have any glue I can borrow?

4. There is a lot of food on the table.

5. Carolina has a new shampoo.

6. Carmen bought a blue shirt for Carlos.

C. Look at Exercise A. Choose two words with the vowel sound /o͞o/. In your notebook, write a sentence for each word.

Grammar 3

Commands

(Please)	Stand up.	Be quiet.
	Don't stand up.	Don't be quiet.
Remember: Give commands with the base form of the verb. Add *please* to be more polite.		

A. Write the numbers 1–8 in your notebook. Then look at the pictures and write the commands from the box.

Stand up.	Don't sit down.	Don't talk.	Raise your hand.
Look up.	Open your book.	Smile.	Close your book.

1. _Don't talk._   2. _____   3. _____   4. _____

5. _____   6. _____   7. _____   8. _____

B. Play a game in small groups. Choose a group leader. The leader says a command ("Sit down" or "Please sit down"). The other players must listen to the leader carefully. If the leader says "Please," the players follow the command. If the leader does *not* say "Please," the players must *not* follow the command. If someone makes a mistake, he or she is out of the game.

Reading

BEFORE YOU READ

Use the learning strategy *Make Inferences* (see page 108).

1. Read the story.
2. When you see a new word, write it in your notebook.
3. Read the sentence that has the word. Then read the two or three sentences before and after that sentence.
4. Guess at the meaning of the new word.
5. Write or draw your guess next to the word in your notebook.

READ THIS!

The Visitors

It is Tuesday afternoon. The sky is gray and cloudy. Carlos is feeling very "blue."

On Sunday, he watched TV all day. On Monday, he watched TV all morning. In the afternoon, Carmen brought him his homework from school, but his mother said, "Rest, Carlos. Don't do your homework now." His father said, "Yes, you need to rest. Do your homework tomorrow." Carlos yawned and said, "Okay. I'm going to sleep."

Now it is Tuesday, and Carlos is very bored. He misses his friends. He thinks to himself, "I'm so bored. Why don't my friends come to visit me?"

Then he hears voices outside his door.

"Is he awake?"

"Maybe he's too tired for visitors."

Carlos wants to leap from his bed. But he cannot. So he shouts, "Come in! Come in! I'm awake. I'm not tired!"

His sister Carmen and his friends Bic, Pablo, and Liliana go into Carlos's room.

"Carlos, are you okay?"

"What happened at the hospital, Carlos?"

Carlos, in a weak voice, says, "Oh, I'm badly hurt. I broke my wrist and sprained my ankle." Carlos shows them the cast on his wrist.

Liliana asks, "Does it hurt?"

Carlos says, "Yes. It hurts *a lot.*"

Liliana says, "Oh, I'm so sorry, Carlos! Here . . . Maria and I made you some cookies."

Bic says, "Samir and I bought you a new CD."

Pablo says, "And I brought my guitar so I can play a new song I wrote."

"Oh," says Carlos weakly. "That's so nice of you . . ."

Carmen says, "You know, I think Carlos is in a lot of pain. We'll come back later, Carlos."

Carlos shouts, "No! I feel great! I'm not in pain. Don't go! Pablo, please play me the song!"

Everyone looks at Carlos. They all start laughing.

Liliana says, "Carlos, you're such an actor!"

AFTER YOU READ

A. Think about the learning strategy.

   1. What inferences did you make about the meanings of new words in the story? Talk about your inferences with the rest of the class.

   2. At the end, Liliana calls Carlos an actor. Why? How did you make this inference?

B. Read **the questions.** Then write the answers in your notebook.

   1. Why is Carlos at home?

   2. What did Carlos do at home?

   3. Did Carlos do his homework on Monday?

   4. Was Carlos awake when his friends came to the door?

   5. What gifts did Carlos's friends bring to him?

Check your work. How many of your answers are correct? Write the number of correct answers in your notebook.

Keep Trying!   Great Work!

Writing

A. You are going to write a dialogue about two people talking on the phone. First, read the dialogue below.

> Bic: Hi, Samir. What are you going to do tomorrow?
>
> Samir: I'm going to go to the movies with my sister. Would you like to come?
>
> Bic: Sure! What are you going to see?
>
> Samir: We're going to see the new George Lucas movie.
>
> Bic: Oh, I want to see that movie. What time are you going to go?
>
> Samir: The show is at two o'clock, so we have to leave my house at one-thirty.
>
> Bic: Okay. See you tomorrow.
>
> Samir: Bye.

B. Read the *Before I Write* checklist. In your notebook, make notes about your weekend plans.

WRITE THIS!

Read the *While I Write* checklist. Look at your notes and write a phone dialogue between you and a friend about your weekend plans. Ask your teacher for new words.

AFTER YOU WRITE

A. Read the *After I Write* checklist. Then check your work.

B. Read your dialogue with a classmate. Read your words and ask your classmate to read the words of your friend. Help your classmate read his or her dialogue.

C. Write a final copy of your dialogue in your notebook.

Tools for Writing

Before I Write

▶ Study the model.

▶ Think about my weekend plans.

▶ Make notes about . . .

  what I am going to do

  where I am going to go

  who I am going to go with

While I Write

▶ Write the names of the speakers at the beginning of what they say.

  Bic: Okay. See you tomorrow.

▶ Use **going to** to ask or tell about the future.

  What are you going to do tomorrow?

  I'm going to go to the movies with my sister.

▶ Use the connecting word **so** to show cause and effect.

  The show is at two o'clock, so we have to leave my house at one-thirty.

After I Write

▶ Did I write the names of the speakers at the beginning of what they say?

▶ Did I use *going to* to ask or tell about the future?

▶ Did I use the connecting word *so* to show cause and effect?

Learning Log

◆ VOCABULARY

Read the words and expressions. Then copy them into your notebook.
Underline the words and expressions you need to review.

Nouns				Expressions
Parts of the Body	*People*	*Other*		Be careful.
	actor	cast	outside	Ouch!
ankle leg	visitor	emergency	pain	See you later.
arm wrist		hospital	race	That sounds like . . .
foot		lesson	voice	

Verbs		Adjectives		Adverbs
break (broke)	shout	awake	fast	weakly
fall (fell)	skate	"blue"	tired	
happen	sleep	bored	weak	
hurt	sprain	cloudy		
leap	visit			
rest	yawn			

◆ LANGUAGE and LEARNING STRATEGIES

Copy the checklist into your notebook. Check what you know. Review what you
need to know.

I can . . .

_____ read and understand the dialogue "The Accident"

_____ ask and answer questions using future with *be going to*

_____ read and use new words with the vowel sound /o͞o/ as in *school*

_____ use the learning strategy *Make Inferences* to learn new words

_____ read and understand the story "The Visitors"

_____ write a dialogue about two people talking about plans

◆ SELF-EVALUATION QUESTIONS

Answer the questions in your notebook.

1. What is easy in Chapter 13? What is difficult in Chapter 13?
2. How can you learn the things that are difficult?

Chapter 14

Hey! The lights went out!

GETTING READY

Look at the picture. What things can you name in English? Say the words. Talk about what is happening in the picture.

LISTENING AND READING

A. Listen to the dialogue. Then answer this question: Why is the principal closing the school for the rest of the day?

B. Read the dialogue.

The Storm

Carlos: Whoa! That's a big storm out there.

Mrs. Kim: Yes, it is. And speaking of storms, let's continue our lesson on weather. Now, yesterday we were talking about . . .

(*Crash!*)

Carmen: Hey! The lights went out!

Maria: Oh! I can't see anything!

Mrs. Kim: Calm down, class. I'm sure the lights will come back on soon. Now, what was I saying? Oh, yes. We were talking about . . .

Carlos: Wow. It sure is dark out there.

Mrs. Kim: Excuse me, Mr. Alvarez. Please take your seat.

Carlos: I'm not sure I can find it!

Students: Ha! ha! ha!
* * * * *

Principal: Good morning, Mrs. Kim. Good morning, students.

Mrs. Kim: Good morning, Mr. Gonzalez.

Principal: The school's electricity is off. A tree fell on the power line. I'm closing the school for the rest of the day. The buses are going to be here soon.
* * * * *

Carlos: Where are those buses? I'm freezing!

Carmen:	Pablo, what were you doing when the lights went out?
Pablo:	I was watching a video in history class. What about you?
Carmen:	I was listening to Mrs. Kim.
Pablo:	Maria, here comes our bus.
Carlos:	Hey, Carmen . . . our bus is behind theirs. Let's go!
Carmen:	Oh, no! I don't have my umbrella!
Maria:	Here, Carmen. You can use mine.
Carmen:	Thanks, Maria!

Pair and Group Work

A. Read the dialogue with a classmate.

B. Act out the dialogue in groups of six.

VOCABULARY

Words		Expressions
storm	soon	Whoa!
continue	electricity	speaking of . . .
weather	power line	It sure is . . .
light	close	Take your seat.
go (went) out	video	I'm freezing!

A. Read and say the vocabulary. Then write the vocabulary in your notebook.

B. Use word analysis to study the vocabulary (see pages 250–251, Steps 1–3).

C. Find the vocabulary in the dialogue. Read the sentences that use the vocabulary.

D. Choose five words from the word box. In your notebook, write five sentences using these words.

Grammar 1

Past Continuous Tense: Statements

Affirmative Statements				Negative Statements			
I	**was**			I	**was not**		
You	**were**			You	**were not**		
He/She It	**was**	**sleeping.**		He/She It	**was not**	**sleeping.**	
We You They	**were**			We You They	**were not**		
Remember: Use the past continuous *to* say what was happening at a specific time in the past.							

was not = wasn't
were not = weren't

Write true affirmative or negative statements in your notebook.
Use the past continuous.

1. I / play soccer / Saturday morning. *I wasn't playing soccer Saturday morning.*
2. It / rain / Sunday afternoon.
3. My teacher / sleep / yesterday in class.
4. I / watch TV / Friday evening.
5. My parents / read the newspaper / last night.

Past Continuous Tense: *Yes/No* Questions

Was	I			you	**were.**		you	**weren't.**
Were	you			I			I	
Was	he/she it	**sleeping?**	Yes,	he/she it	**was.**	No,	he/she it	**wasn't.**
Were	we you they			you we they	**were.**		you we they	**weren't.**

Look at your answers in the previous exercise. In your notebook, write a question for each answer.

EXAMPLE: *Were you playing soccer Saturday morning?*

Grammar 2

Past Continuous Tense: Information Questions

What was Pablo **doing**?	He was watching a video.
When was he **watching** the video?	He was watching it yesterday.
Where was he **watching** it?	He was watching it in history class.
Who was he **watching** it with?	He was watching it with his classmates.
What else was he **doing**?	He was taking some notes.

A. Look at the picture. The lights just went out at David's house. Write questions about David in your notebook. Use the question words in parentheses.

1. He was playing a game. (What) *What was David doing?*
2. He was playing a game last night. (When)
3. He was playing in the living room. (Where)
4. He was playing with his sister. (Who/with)
5. He was eating popcorn. (What else/do)

B. Work with a classmate. Ask and answer questions about where David's mother and father were and what they were doing when the lights went out.

Word Study

Other Vowel Sound: /o͝o/

The letters *oo* can stand for the vowel sound /o͝o/ as in *look*.

A. Use the learning strategy *Sound Out* (see page 32) and the pictures to read the words.

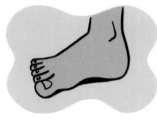

1. notebook

2. good-bye

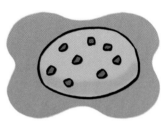

3. cookie

4. foot

5. hook

6. cook

B. Read the sentences aloud. Then copy them into your notebook. Circle the letters that stand for the vowel sound /o͝o/.

1. Did Carlos hurt his foot?

2. Carolina and Carmen were baking cookies yesterday.

3. Is this Liliana's notebook?

4. There are two fish on Pablo's hook.

5. What are they going to cook for dinner?

6. Pedro is saying good-bye to Samir.

C. Look at Exercise A. Choose two words with the vowel sound /o͝o/. In your notebook, write a sentence for each word.

Grammar 3

Possessive Pronouns

Possessive Adjectives		Possessive Pronouns
It's **my** book.	→	It's **mine**.
It's **your** book.	→	It's **yours**.
It's **his** book.	→	It's **his**.
It's **her** book.	→	It's **hers**.
It's **our** book.	→	It's **ours**.
It's **their** book.	→	It's **theirs**.

Copy the sentences into your notebook. Then fill in the blanks with the correct possessive pronoun.

1. Those umbrellas are _____*theirs*_____. (their umbrellas)
2. This money is _____. (her money)
3. That house is _____. (our house)
4. This calculator is _____. (my calculator)
5. These pens are _____. (your pens)

Questions with *whose*

Whose book is that? It's **mine**.
Whose pens are those? They're **hers**.

A. Look at the sentences in the previous exercise. Write questions and answers about them in your notebook.
EXAMPLE: *Whose umbrellas are those? They're theirs.*

B. Read the conversation. Then listen.

A: There's a dollar bill on the table. Whose is it?
B: It's mine.
A: I don't think so. I think it's Mi-Sun's.
B: No, it's not hers. It's mine.
C: What are you two talking about? That's my money.
A: Ha! I knew it wasn't yours, Koji.

C. Practice the conversation in Exercise B with two of your classmates. Then make new conversations using your own information.

BEFORE YOU READ

As you read, use the learning strategy *Use Selective Attention* (see page 66) to answer this question: What did Carlos and Carmen's mother not want them to do?

READ THIS!

There was no electricity at Washington School for two days. The school was closed. The students had to stay home.

On the second day, it was still raining. Carmen and Carlos's mother said, "It's a perfect day to do your homework."

But Carmen and Carlos did not think so. They were not doing their homework. Instead, they were watching TV.

Their mother did not think this was a good idea. She said, "Turn off the TV. Don't you know it's dangerous to watch TV or talk on the phone during bad weather?"

"But Mom," said Carlos. "It's only raining outside. Isn't it only dangerous to watch TV or talk on the phone during a thunderstorm?"

"Hmm. I guess so," said their mother. But she really did not want them to watch so much TV. She had a plan. She said, "You can help me clean the house. Go and clean your bedrooms."

Carlos did not want to clean his room. His broken wrist was hurting. "Mom," he said. "My wrist is hurting. Can I do my homework instead?"

Carmen said, "And mine is clean. Can I please call one of my friends and talk on the phone?"

Carlos's mother was happy that Carlos was going to do his homework. She said, "Yes, Carlos, you can do your homework. And Carmen, you can clean Carlos's room for him."

Carmen was not happy, but she cleaned Carlos's room.

Later, their mother was cooking dinner. Carlos came into the kitchen. "Mom," he said, "I finished my homework." Carmen came in the kitchen, too. "Mom," she said, "I cleaned his room."

"Good," her mother said. "Carmen, you can do your homework after dinner."

The rain was ending. After dinner, the rain stopped completely. Carmen did not want to do her homework. Instead, she decided to talk on the phone with Liliana.

The next day was Saturday. It was sunny and beautiful. The weather was nice, so Carlos went to the park with his friends. But Carmen did not go with them. On this very beautiful day, she was in her room. She was doing her homework!

AFTER YOU READ

A. Did you use the learning strategy *Use Selective Attention* to find the answer to the question in *Before You Read*? Find the sentence in the story that answers the question. Discuss your answer with a classmate.

B. True or false? In your notebook, write *True* or *False* for each statement. For your *False* answers, make the sentences correct. Write *I don't know* if the information is *not* in the reading.

1. Carlos and Carmen's mother doesn't like TV.
2. Carmen and Carlos wanted to clean their rooms.
3. Finally, Carlos did his homework and Carmen cleaned Carlos's room.
4. After dinner, Carmen did her homework.
5. On Saturday, Carmen watched TV.

Check your work. How many of your answers are correct? Write the number of correct answers in your notebook.

Writing

A. You are going to write a paragraph about something that happened to you. First, read the paragraph below.

> When I was seven years old, I rode my bicycle every day. I rode in the park and on the street in every kind of weather. One day I was riding with my friend Carlos. We were going fast. I was talking to Carlos when a big dog jumped in front of my bike. I hit the brake hard and fell. My arm was hurting. A woman came over to help me. Carlos said, "He almost hit that dog." She said, "Yes, I know. The dog is mine." Then the woman called my mom. My mom came and took me to the hospital. My arm was in a cast for six weeks.

B. Read the *Before I Write* checklist. In your notebook, make notes about something that happened to you. Describe when, where, and how it happened.

WRITE THIS!

Read the *While I Write* checklist. Look at your notes and write a paragraph about something that happened to you. Ask your teacher for new words.

AFTER YOU WRITE

A. Read the *After I Write* checklist. Then check your work.

B. Read your paragraph to a classmate. Listen to your classmate read his or her paragraph.

C. Write a final copy of your paragraph in your notebook.

Tools for Writing

Before I Write

▶ Study the model.

▶ Think about something that happened to me.

▶ Make notes about . . .

    when it happened
    where it happened
    how it happened

While I Write

▶ Use *was* or *were* and an **–ing** word to tell what people were doing when the event happened.

One day I was riding with my friend Carlos.

▶ Use the **simple past** to tell about the event and what happened next.

I was talking to Carlos when a big dog jumped in front of my bike.

▶ Use **quotation marks** around the exact words that a person says.

She said, "Yes, I know."

After I Write

▶ Did I use *was* or *were* and an –ing word to tell what people were doing when the event happened?

▶ Did I use the simple past to tell about the event and what happened next?

▶ Did I use quotation marks around the exact words that a person says?

Learning Log

◆ VOCABULARY

Read the words and expressions. Then copy them into your notebook.
Underline the words and expressions you need to review.

Nouns		Expressions
Climate-Related	**Other**	I'm freezing!
rain	electricity	I guess so.
storm	light	It sure is . . .
thunderstorm	plan	speaking of . . .
weather	power line	Take your seat.
	video	Whoa!

Verbs		Adjectives		Adverbs
close	end	broken	perfect	completely
continue	go (went) out	dangerous	sunny	instead
				soon

◆ LANGUAGE and LEARNING STRATEGIES

Copy the checklist into your notebook. Check what you know. Review what you
need to know.

I can . . .

_____ read and understand the dialogue "The Storm"

_____ ask and answer questions using the past continuous

_____ use possessive pronouns correctly

_____ read and use new words with the vowel sound /o͞o/ as in *look*

_____ use the learning strategy *Use Selective Attention* to find key ideas

_____ read and understand the story "Mother's Plan"

_____ write a paragraph about something that happened to me

◆ SELF-EVALUATION QUESTIONS

Answer the questions in your notebook.

1. What is easy in Chapter 14? What is difficult in Chapter 14?

2. How can you learn the things that are difficult?

Chapter 15

We'll have a study group.

Look at the picture. What things can you name in English? Say the words. Talk about what is happening in the picture.

A. Listen to the dialogue. Then answer this question: What can the students do to get ready for the exam?

B. Read the dialogue.

Help for Maria

Bic:	It was fun staying home from school for a few days.
Samir:	Yeah, but now we have a lot of work to catch up on.
Carlos:	And you know what that means. It means Mr. Gomez might give us extra homework!

* * * * *

Mr. Gomez:	Class, we need to talk about our final exam in reading.
Maria:	Reading? A reading test?
Mr. Gomez:	Yes, Maria, a reading test.
Maria:	But I can't read!
Mr. Gomez:	Of course you can read.
Maria:	But I'm bad at taking exams. I get really nervous.

Samir:	Don't worry, Maria. I'll help you get ready for the exam.
Bic:	I will, too.
Carmen:	And so will I.
Mr. Gomez:	That gives me an idea. Why don't you have a study group?
Carmen:	That's a good idea, Mr. Gomez. That'll help Maria and everyone.
Mr. Gomez:	What do you think, Maria?
Maria:	I guess it might help, but . . .
Mr. Gomez:	Okay, everyone. Please ask your parents to come to a meeting tomorrow night. We'll make plans for the study group.

Mei:	Mr. Gomez, may I ask my grandmother to come, too?
Mr. Gomez:	Of course, Mei.
Carmen:	What else can we do to get ready for the exam?
Mr. Gomez:	Well, you can study the vocabulary words and review the stories in our book. Try to read one story every day. Read, read, read.
Maria:	Oh, no. I can't.
Everyone:	Yes, you can, Maria!

Pair and Group Work

A. Read the dialogue with a classmate.

B. Act out the dialogue in groups of seven.

VOCABULARY

Words		Expressions
a few	group	catch up
extra	meeting	bad at
final	review	of course
exam	try	

A. Read and say the vocabulary. Then write the vocabulary in your notebook.

B. Use word analysis to study the vocabulary (see pages 250–251, Steps 1–3).

C. Find the vocabulary in the dialogue. Read the sentences that use the vocabulary.

D. Choose five words from the word box. In your notebook, write five questions using these words. Ask a classmate your questions. Answer your classmate's questions.

Grammar 1

Future Tense with *will*: Statements

Affirmative Statements			Negative Statements		
I You He/She We You They	**will**	help her.	I You He/She We You They	**will not**	help her.
Remember: Use *will* future to talk about (1) a sudden idea you have or (2) promises or refusals. Use the base form of the verb after *will* or *won't*.					

I will	= I'll	we will	= we'll
he will	= he'll	you will	= you'll
she will	= she'll	they will	= they'll

will not = won't

Copy the sentences into your notebook. Then fill in the blanks. Use *I'll* or *I won't*.

1. I'm hungry, so ___*I'll*___ make a sandwich.
2. I'm sick, so _*I won't*_ go to the movies today.
3. It's raining, so _____ get my umbrella.
4. It's hot, so _____ wear a coat.
5. I'm thirsty, so _____ get some lemonade.

Future Tense with *will*: Yes/No Questions

Will	I you he/she we you they	see her?	Yes,	you I he/she you we they	**will.**	No,	you I he/she you we they	**won't.**

On New Year's Day, people make promises. Write *yes/no* questions for these statements in your notebook. Then ask a classmate the questions.

1. I will study harder. *Will you study harder?*
2. I will keep my room cleaner.
3. I will go to bed earlier.
4. I will speak English a lot.
5. I will do homework every afternoon.

Grammar 2

Future Tense with *will*: Information Questions

Who will bring snacks to the study group?	Maria **will bring** snacks.
What will Maria **bring**?	She**'ll bring** some popcorn.
What else will she **bring**?	She**'ll bring** some empanadas, too.
What kind of empanadas **will** she **bring**?	She**'ll bring** homemade empanadas.
Where will she **get** homemade empanadas?	She**'ll get** them from home.

A. Match each question in the left-hand column with an answer from the right-hand column. Write the letter of the correct answer in your notebook.

   _c_   **1.** What will Sophie bring?
   _____ **2.** Who will bring sandwiches?
   _____ **3.** Where will they get cookies?
   _____ **4.** What kind of ice cream will you bring?
   _____ **5.** What else will you bring?

  a. I'll bring chocolate ice cream.
  b. They'll get them from the market.
  c. She'll bring lemonade and soda.
  d. I'll bring some carrots, too.
  e. Samir will bring them.

B. Read the conversation. Then listen.

A: I'll bring some snacks to our study group tonight.

B: Great. What kind of snacks will you bring?

A: I'll bring homemade empanadas.

B: Where will you get homemade empanadas?

A: Don't you know what "homemade" means?

C. Practice the conversation in Exercise B with a classmate. Then make new conversations with your own information.

Word Study

Other Vowel Sound: /ô/

The letters *au* and *aw* can stand for the vowel sound /ô/ as in *auditorium* and *saw*.

A. Use the learning strategy *Sound Out* (see page 32) and the pictures to read the words.

1. August

2. author

3. audience

4. autumn

5. yawn

6. draw

7. straw

8. paw

B. Read the sentences aloud. Then copy them into your notebook. Circle the letters that stand for the vowel sound /ô/.

1. What did she draw today?

2. The audience really liked the show.

3. I need a straw for my soda, please.

4. What are you going to do in August?

5. She yawned at the end of the movie.

6. Our cat hurt its paw.

C. Look at Exercise A. Choose two words with the vowel sound /ô/. In your notebook, write a sentence for each word.

Grammar 3

Statements with *may* and *might*

Affirmative Statements			Negative Statements		
I You He/She We You They	**may** **might**	give them homework.	I You He/She We You They	**may not** **might not**	give them homework.
Remember: Use *may* or *might* to talk about possible plans for the future.					

A. Pablo and Bic are talking about weekend plans. Pablo has possible plans. Bic has definite plans. Write the dialogue in your notebook. Use *be going to, may,* and *might* at least once each.

> **Bic:** What are you going to do this weekend?
>
> **Pablo:** I (**1**) ___*might*___ go swimming. (affirmative)
> And I (**2**) _____ go shopping with my mom. (affirmative) But I
> (**3**) _____ buy anything. (negative) And I (**4**) _____ study on
> Sunday afternoon. (affirmative)
>
> **Bic:** You're lucky. I (**5**) _____ stay home and study all
> weekend. (affirmative)

B. Write six sentences in your notebook about your weekend plans. Use *be going to, may,* and *might* at least once each. Then tell a classmate about your plans.

Reading

Use the learning strategy *Personalize*. As you read, ask yourself the following questions:

1. How does Mei feel about her grandmother? Would I feel the same way?
2. What does Mei think about doing? Would I think about the same things?

READ THIS!

Grandmother Chu

My name is Mei. I live with my father, two sisters, three brothers, and my grandmother. My grandmother is seventy-five years old. At night, she tells me stories about her life in China. She tells her stories in Chinese. Then sometimes she holds my chin and looks into my eyes. She says, "Your eyes are my home." I love my grandmother very much.

Yesterday I told my grandmother about the meeting at school. She looked sad and said, "I can't go. My English is so bad." I told her there is a teacher who speaks Chinese. "She will translate everything into Chinese," I said.

Then my grandmother's eyes lit up. "Okay. I will go to school with you!"

This evening, my grandmother and I went to the meeting at school. All my friends were there with their mothers or fathers.

My grandmother whispered in my ear, "Mei, I always wanted to go to school! Now I am here. School is such a lovely place."

"Oh, Grandmother, you never went to school?"

"I had to work. I had to help my family."

"But you know how to read in Chinese. How did you learn?"

"Your mother taught me."

"My mother?"

Then Mr. Gomez started to talk. The translators spoke softly in Spanish, Chinese, and Vietnamese. I thought about how I wanted to do well on the exams. I thought about making my grandmother proud.

Mr. Gomez said, "Parents, we need your help. Your children will do well on their exams, but they may need extra time to study. Can you help?"

I looked at my grandmother. She was nodding her head. I raised my hand. I said, "My grandmother has something to say."

Mr. Gomez said, "Please go ahead, Mrs. Chu."

My grandmother spoke in Chinese, and Mrs. Wong translated for her into English. She said, "Mei and her friends can study in my home. I will make cookies and good Chinese food for them. Please come to my home."

Mr. Gomez thanked my grandmother. "Your idea is wonderful. The study group will meet in your home."

My grandmother was smiling. She said to me quietly, "Yes, I will have a study group for you and your friends."

AFTER YOU READ

A. Think about the learning strategy. As you read the story, did you think about what Mei was feeling? Would you feel the same way? Discuss your answers with a classmate.

B. Read the questions. Then write the answers in your notebook.

1. What kind of stories does Mei's grandmother tell her?
2. Mei learned two new things about her grandmother. What did she learn?
3. Mei's grandmother doesn't speak English well. How did she understand what Mr. Gomez was saying?
4. What will Mei's grandmother do for Mei and her friends?

Check your work. How many of your answers are correct? Write the number of correct answers in your notebook.

Writing

A. You are going to write a few paragraphs about one of your goals. First, read the paragraphs below.

> I want to be more successful in school. Here are some ways I can reach my goal:
> 1. I'll read more books. I'll try to read one book a week.
> 2. I'll speak up more in class and ask more questions.
> 3. I'll do my homework right after school.
> The easiest step for me will be to read one book a week. I love to read! The hardest step for me will be to speak up more in class. It makes me nervous. But I know it is important.

B. Read the *Before I Write* checklist. In your notebook, make notes about some steps you can take to reach your goal.

WRITE THIS!

Read the *While I Write* checklist. Look at your notes and write a few paragraphs about one of your goals and how you plan to reach it. Ask your teacher for new words.

AFTER YOU WRITE

A. Read the *After I Write* checklist. Then check your work.

B. Read your paragraphs to a classmate. Listen to your classmate read his or her paragraphs.

C. Write a final copy of your paragraphs in your notebook.

Before I Write

▶ Study the model.

▶ Think about one of my goals for the future.

▶ Make notes on how I can reach my goal.

While I Write

▶ Make a step-by-step list for reaching my goal.

▶ Say which step will be the easiest and which step will be the hardest.

> *The easiest step for me will be to read one book a week.*

▶ Use **will** or its contraction **'ll** with a verb to talk about the future.

> *I'll read more books.*

After I Write

▶ Did I make a step-by-step list for reaching my goal?

▶ Did I say which step will be the easiest and which step will be the hardest?

▶ Did I use *will* or its contraction *'ll* with a verb to talk about the future?

Learning Log

◆ VOCABULARY

Read the vocabulary words and expressions. Then copy them into your notebook. Underline the words and expressions you need to review.

Nouns					Expressions
Parts of the Body	**Language**	**Other**			bad at
	Vietnamese				catch up
chin		exam	meeting		of course
ear		group	translator		
eye		life			

Verbs		Adjectives		Adverbs	
go ahead	review	a few	lovely	softly	
hold	translate	extra	proud	quietly	
light (lit) up	try	final			
nod	whisper				

◆ LANGUAGE and LEARNING STRATEGIES

Copy the checklist into your notebook. Check what you know. Review what you need to know.

I can . . .

_____ read and understand the dialogue "Help for Maria"

_____ ask and answer questions using future with *will*

_____ use *may* and *might* to express possibility

_____ read and use new words with the vowel sound /ô/ as in *saw* and *auditorium*

_____ use the learning strategy *Personalize* to understand how a character feels, thinks, and acts

_____ read and understand the story "Grandmother Chu"

_____ write a few paragraphs about one of my goals for the future

◆ SELF-EVALUATION QUESTIONS

Answer the questions in your notebook.

1. What is easy in Chapter 15? What is difficult in Chapter 15?
2. How can you learn the things that are difficult?

GOALS
In Unit 6 you will learn to . . .

- **listen to and read dialogues and stories about students studying together and helping each other with their problems**

- **ask and answer questions about how often you do things**

- **give advice, make suggestions, and give reasons**

- **study words with other vowel sounds**

- **write about a classmate's hobby or interest, give advice to someone, and write a story**

- **use the learning strategies** *Use What You Know, Use Selective Attention,* **and** *Make Predictions*

Chapter 16

I sometimes study with my friends.

GETTING READY

Look at the picture. What things can you name in English? Say the words. Talk about what is happening in the picture.

LISTENING AND READING

A. Listen to the dialogue. Then answer this question: When does Sophie have dance class?

B. Read the dialogue.

The Study Group

Carlos: Hi, everyone! I'm sorry I'm late. Soccer practice went a little longer than it usually does.

Pablo: It's okay, Carlos. We just started.

Maria: What were you doing at soccer practice? Your wrist is still broken.

Carlos: I sometimes help the coach.

Pablo: You know, I really like having a study group.

Carlos: Me, too. And I especially like studying at Mei's house.

Mei: You do? Why?

Carlos: I like eating the snacks your grandmother makes for us.

Carmen: Typical Carlos. He's always thinking about food!

Maria: Listen . . . do you mind if we start studying? I'm really worried about the English test.

Carmen: Maria, stop worrying so much. You're going to get gray hair, like my grandmother!

Mei: Why *are* you so worried, Maria?

Maria: Oh, Mei, you know. I have such a hard time with English. Especially with reading.

Carmen: Studying helps, right? How often do you study? I study about three times a week.

Maria:	Well . . . you're good in English, Carmen. I have to study every day! And it's *still* hard for me.
Carlos:	Wait. Where's Sophie? Isn't she coming to the study group?
Mei:	That's a good question.
Carmen:	Sophie has dance class every afternoon. She told me she'll be here later.
Maria:	I hope so. Or she'll miss the chance to study with us.
Carlos:	That's right . . . and she'll miss the great snacks!

Pair and Group Work

A. Read the dialogue with a classmate.

B. Act out the dialogue in groups of five.

VOCABULARY

Words		Expressions
practice	typical	Do you mind if . . . ?
coach	tell (told)	a hard time
especially	chance	I hope so.

A. Read and say the vocabulary. Then write the vocabulary in your notebook.

B. Use word analysis to study the vocabulary (see pages 250-251, Steps 1–3).

C. Find the vocabulary in the dialogue. Read the sentences that use the vocabulary.

D. Choose five words from the box. In your notebook, write five sentences using these words.

Adverbs of Frequency

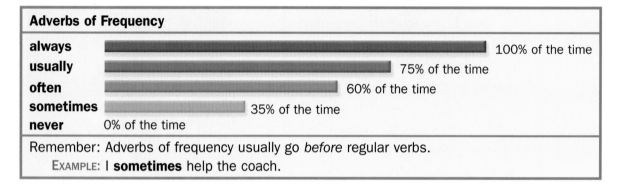

Adverbs of Frequency		
always		100% of the time
usually		75% of the time
often		60% of the time
sometimes		35% of the time
never		0% of the time
Remember: Adverbs of frequency usually go *before* regular verbs.		
EXAMPLE: I **sometimes** help the coach.		

Add the adverbs of frequency in parentheses to the sentences. Write them in your notebook.

1. Sophie eats dinner at six. (usually)   *Sophie usually eats dinner at six.*
2. Carlos and Carmen study together. (sometimes)
3. Maria worries about tests. (always)
4. Mei and Sophie think about Paco. (often)
5. Pablo goes to bed early. (never)

Adverbs of Frequency with *be*

I	am		
He/She/It	is	**sometimes**	late.
We/You/They	are		
Remember: Adverbs of frequency usually go *after be*.			

Make true statements about yourself using adverbs of frequency. Write them in your notebook. Then read your sentences to a classmate.

1. I'm hungry after school.
   I'm usually hungry after school.
2. I'm tired in the morning.
3. I'm late.
4. I'm a good student.
5. I'm silly.

Grammar 2

How often and Expressions of Frequency

How often does your study group meet?	It meets	one time *or* once	a day.
		two times *or* twice	a week.
		three times	a month.
		four times	a year.

A. Make true sentences about yourself using expressions of frequency. Write them in your notebook. (If you *never* do something, write that.)

1. I clean my room.   *I clean my room once a month.*
2. I eat fruit.
3. I go to the movies.
4. I drink milk.
5. I go shopping.

B. Work with a classmate. Ask and answer questions about the activities in Exercise A using *how often*.

EXAMPLE: *How often do you clean your room?*

C. Work with a classmate. Ask and answer questions about the activities below using *how often*.

EXAMPLE: *How often do you eat hamburgers?*

go swimming
go out to eat
make your bed
drink orange juice
help cook dinner
eat hamburgers
wash the dishes
buy CDs
get sick
buy candy
play computer games
eat fish

Word Study

Other Vowel Sound: /oi/

> The letters *oi* and *oy* can stand for the vowel sound /oi/ as in *voice* and *enjoy*.

A. Use the learning strategy *Sound Out* (see page 32) and the pictures to read the words.

1. soil

2. boil

3. coin

4. oil

5. point

6. toy

7. Roy

8. boy

B. Read the sentences aloud. Then copy them into your notebook.
Circle the letters that stand for the vowel sound /oi/.

1. Is Roy a new student in your class?

2. I like finding old coins.

3. The water in the pot is boiling.

4. The boys are playing in the gym.

5. Did Sophie buy a toy for the new baby?

6. You need to put more oil in the pan.

C. Look at Exercise A. Choose two words with the vowel sound /oi/.
In your notebook, write a sentence for each word.

Grammar 3

Gerunds as Objects of Verbs

> Gerunds (base form of verb + *ing*) are verbs that act like nouns. The verbs
> *love, enjoy, like, hate, stop, start,* and *finish* can be followed by gerunds.
>
> EXAMPLES: I like **cooking**.
> _(gerund)_
>
> He loves **painting**.
> _(gerund)_
>
> Please start **reading** now.
> _(gerund)_

A. In your notebook, write how you feel about these activities. Use *love, enjoy, like, don't like,* or *hate* plus gerunds.

1. study math   *I enjoy studying math.*
2. cook
3. go shopping
4. play sports
5. take tests

B. In your notebook, write five sentences about things you like and don't like doing. Use each of these words once: *love, enjoy, like, don't like, hate.* Use gerunds. Then read your sentences to a classmate.

C. Read the conversation. Then listen.

A: I enjoy painting. I paint all the time.
B: I can tell. You're very good.
A: Oh. Thank you!
B: I don't like painting very much. I like drawing.

D. Practice the conversation in Exercise C with a classmate. Then make new conversations using your own information.

Reading

BEFORE YOU READ

Use the learning strategy *Use What You Know* (see page 98).

1. Look at the pictures and the title of the story. Who is this story about?
2. Discuss with a classmate what you already know about this person. Do not look at the story.
3. Think about and use the learning strategy *Use What You Know* to help you read the story.

READ THIS!

The Dancer

Sophie is a student at Washington School. She is a friendly, intelligent girl who has a lot of friends and enjoys school.

Sophie loves dancing. When she lived in Haiti, her town sometimes had festivals or celebrations. The festivals happened two or three times a year. Sophie usually danced in the festivals with her friends and relatives. They often got together at Sophie's aunt's house to practice their dances. It was so much fun. Sophie says, "Dancing in the festivals is one of my favorite memories of my life in Haiti."

Now Sophie is in a dance club at the town recreation center. It is her favorite free-time activity. "I really like being in a club, and I like my dance teacher, Ms. Morgan. She's very nice, and she teaches me a lot of new things about dancing.

Sophie is a very good dancer. She makes dancing look easy. Sophie says, "It might look easy, but it's harder than it looks. *Much* harder." Sophie sometimes tells her friends, including the boys, that they should try taking dance classes. "It's fun, and it's great exercise," she says.

Sophie usually goes to dance club every afternoon. However, right now she has a problem with her schedule. Her friends have a study group three times a week at Mei's house. She wants to join them, but it is difficult for her to go to the study group because she needs time to do her house chores and homework.

Sophie says, "My mom says dancers have to have good balance, but students have to have good balance, too. She says students have to balance school and fun. She's probably right."

Sophie does not want to stop going to dance club, but she plans to start going only three times a week. The other two days she will go to the study group. She really wants to do well on the final exam. "Plus," says Sophie, "I sometimes get bored studying by myself. I like being with other people when I study."

AFTER YOU READ

A. Think about the learning strategy. What information did you know about Sophie before reading? Did this information help you read? What new information did you get from this reading? Discuss your answers with a classmate.

B. True or false? In your notebook, write *True* or *False* for each statement. For your *False* answers, make the sentences correct. Write *I don't know* if the information is *not* in the reading.

1. Sophie enjoyed dancing in festivals in Haiti.
2. Sophie thinks dancing is difficult.
3. Her friends don't want to take dance classes.
4. She will start going to dance club three days a week.
5. Sophie likes studying by herself.

Check your work. How many of your answers are correct? Write the number of correct answers in your notebook.

Keep Trying!   Great Work!

Writing

BEFORE YOU WRITE

A. You are going to write a paragraph about a classmate's hobby or interest. First, read the paragraph below.

> My classmate Julia likes playing chess. She practices every day. She plays in chess tournaments two or three times a year. She often wins, but not always. She says, "I like to play with my grandfather after school. He likes teaching me about the game, and I like learning from him. He usually wins, but sometimes he lets me win."

B. Read the *Before I Write* checklist. As a class, write five to ten questions that you can ask each other. Write the questions in your notebook.

C. Use the questions you wrote in Exercise B to interview a classmate about his or her hobby or interest. Write the answers in your notebook.

WRITE THIS!

Read the *While I Write* checklist. Look at your notes and write a paragraph about your classmate's hobby or interest in your notebook. Ask your teacher for new words.

AFTER YOU WRITE

A. Read the *After I Write* checklist. Check your work.

B. Read your paragraph to your classmate and check your information. Read your classmate's paragraph about you and check your classmate's information.

C. Write a final copy of your paragraph in your notebook. Then make a copy and give it to your classmate.

Tools for Writing

Before I Write

▶ Study the model.

▶ Write interview questions about hobbies or interests.

▶ Interview a classmate.

▶ Make notes on my classmate's answers.

While I Write

▶ Use **–ing** words to describe something my classmate likes to do.

  My classmate Julia likes playing chess.

▶ Use words and phrases that tell **exactly how often** something happens.

  She practices every day.

▶ Use **adverbs of frequency** to tell how often something happens.

  She often wins, but not always.

After I Write

▶ Did I use –ing words to describe something my classmate likes to do?

▶ Did I use words and phrases that tell exactly how often something happens?

▶ Did I use adverbs of frequency to tell how often something happens?

Learning Log

◆ VOCABULARY

Read the words and expressions. Then copy them into your notebook.
Underline the words and expressions you need to review.

Nouns				Expressions
People	**Other**			a hard time
coach	activity	chore	memory	Do you mind if . . .
dancer	balance	club	practice	get (got) together
myself	celebration	exercise	recreation center	I hope so.
relatives	chance	festival	town	

Verbs		Adjectives	Adverb
balance	plan	friendly	especially
enjoy	practice	intelligent	
include	tell (told)	typical	
join			

◆ LANGUAGE and LEARNING STRATEGIES

Copy the checklist into your notebook. Check what you know. Review what you
need to know.

I can . . .

_____ read and understand the dialogue "The Study Group"

_____ ask and answer questions about how often someone does something

_____ ask and answer questions using gerunds

_____ read and use new words with the vowel sound /oi/ as in *voice*

_____ use the learning strategy *Use What You Know* to understand new
information

_____ read and understand the story "The Dancer"

_____ write a paragraph about my classmate's hobby or interest

◆ SELF-EVALUATION QUESTIONS

Answer the questions in your notebook.

1. What is easy in Chapter 16? What is difficult in Chapter 16?
2. How can you learn the things that are difficult?

Chapter 17

You should get some rest.

Look at the picture. What things can you name in English? Say the words. Talk about what is happening in the picture.

A. Listen to the dialogue. Then answer this question: Will Maria go home today?

B. Read the dialogue.

At the Nurse's Office

Maria:	Mr. Gomez . . . I . . . umm . . .
Mr. Gomez:	Yes, Maria.
Maria:	I feel terrible.
Mr. Gomez:	You do? Okay, Maria. You should go see Ms. Cho. Carmen, please walk with Maria to the nurse's office.
Carmen:	Sure.
Sophie:	Feel better, Maria.
Maria:	Thanks.

* * * * *

Ms. Cho:	Okay. Tell me how you feel.
Maria:	I have a sore throat, a stomachache, and a bad headache.
Ms. Cho:	Hmm. Tell me, Maria, how is Mr. Gomez's class?
Maria:	What? Oh . . . it's very hard.
Ms: Cho:	English *is* a hard class . . . Maria, you're going to be fine.
Maria:	Is that all?
Ms. Cho:	You should get a lot of rest and drink plenty of water.
Maria:	Shouldn't I take some medicine?
Ms. Cho:	Not today. But call a doctor tomorrow . . . if you don't feel better.
Maria:	Shouldn't I stay home for a couple of days?
Ms. Cho:	You should go home today because you're sick. But you could come to school tomorrow . . . if you feel better.

Maria:	Okay.
Ms. Cho:	Now, rest here on the bed until your mother gets here. Okay?
Maria:	Okay. Thank you, Ms. Cho.
Ms. Cho:	You're welcome. Oh, and by the way, Maria, I'm curious . . . do you have a test tomorrow in Mr. Gomez's class?
Maria:	Well . . . umm . . . yes, I do.
Ms. Cho:	I see.

Pair and Group Work

A. Read the dialogue with a classmate.

B. Act out the dialogue in groups of five.

VOCABULARY

Words		Expressions
terrible	plenty	Feel better.
nurse	medicine	a couple of (days)
office	doctor	By the way, . . .
sore throat	stay	
stomachache	curious	
headache		

A. Read and say the vocabulary. Then write the vocabulary in your notebook.

B. Use word analysis to study the vocabulary (see pages 250-251, Steps 1–3).

C. Find the vocabulary in the dialogue. Read the sentences that use the vocabulary.

D. Group words that go together. Write these headings in your notebook: Feelings; Illnesses; Occupations; Verbs; Other Words. Find the new words in the dialogue that go in each of these groups. Write them in your notebook.

Grammar 1

Statements with *should*

Affirmative Statements			Negative Statements		
I, You, He/She, We, You, They	**should**	sit down.	I, You, He/She, We, You, They	**should not**	sit down.
Remember: Use *should* to give strong advice. Use the plain form of the verb after *should*.					

should not = shouldn't

Write affirmative or negative statements about Maria in your notebook. Use *should* or *shouldn't*.

1. get a lot of rest *Maria should get a lot of rest.*
2. walk home
3. stay in bed
4. go swimming
5. drink plenty of water

Yes/No Questions with *should*

Should Shouldn't	I you he/she we you they	see Ms. Cho, too?	Yes,	you I he/she you we they	should. shouldn't.	No,	you I he/she you we they	shouldn't.

A. Imagine you're at the nurse's office. Write *yes/no* questions in your notebook. Use *should* for general advice. Use *shouldn't* when you want the nurse to say *yes*.

1. take medicine *Should I take medicine?*
2. go home
3. call a doctor
4. go to school tomorrow
5. drink plenty of soda

B. Work with a classmate. Do a role play about visiting the school nurse. The student should ask questions, and the nurse should give advice.

Grammar 2

Statements with *can* and *could* for Possibility

I, You, He/She, We, You, They	**could**	come to school tomorrow.
Remember: Use *could* to make suggestions. *Could* is weaker than *should*.		

A. Match the problems in items 1–5 with the suggestions in the box. Write sentences with *could* in your notebook.

make a sandwich	study more	drink some soda
rest a while	go to the movies	

1. I'm worried about the test. *You could study more.*
2. I'm thirsty.
3. I'm tired.
4. I'm bored.
5. I'm hungry.

B. Read the conversation. Then listen.

A: I'm bored.

B: We could go to a movie.

A: A movie?

B: Yeah.

C. Practice the conversation in Exercise B with a classmate. Then make new conversations with your own information. Begin with *I'm bored, I'm hungry,* or *I'm thirsty.*

Word Study

Other Vowel Sound: /ou/

The letters *ou* and *ow* can stand for the vowel sound /ou/ as in *out* and *now*.

A. Use the learning strategy *Sound Out* (see page 32) and the pictures to read the words.

1. cloud

2. house

3. round

4. mouse

5. eyebrow

6. crowd

7. brown

8. town

B. Read the sentences aloud. Then copy them into your notebook. Circle the letters that stand for the vowel sound /ou/.

1. We saw a huge gray cloud in the sky.

2. She has a brown cat.

3. There was a big crowd at the game.

4. She read her grandson a story about a mouse.

5. We're going to go shopping in your town tomorrow.

6. You can study at my house after school today.

C. Look at Exercise A. Choose two words with the vowel sound /ou/. In your notebook, write a sentence for each word.

Grammar 3

Because Clauses

> Maria should go home. She is sick.
> ——► Maria should go home **because** she is sick.

> Remember: Use *because* clauses to give reasons.
> Use pronouns in the *because* clause.

A. Make one sentence each from the pairs of sentences below. Write the sentences in your notebook.

1. Bic likes video games. He thinks video games are exciting.
   Bic likes video games because he thinks they're exciting.
2. Sophie hates soccer. She thinks soccer is boring.
3. Liliana likes love stories. She thinks love stories are interesting.
4. Carlos doesn't like math. He thinks math is hard.

B. In your notebook, write sentences that give your own opinion about these subjects and the reasons for your opinion. Use *love, like, enjoy, don't like,* or *hate.*

EXAMPLE: *I like roller coasters because I think they're fun.*

1. roller coasters
2. dancing
3. love stories
4. video games
5. math
6. watching TV

C. Play a game in small groups. Use the topics in Exercise B. The first person makes a statement (*I don't like love stories because I think they're boring*). The next person adds his or her own statement (*Flavio doesn't like love stories because he thinks they're boring. I enjoy math because . . .*). Each person adds to the list. If someone makes a mistake, he or she is out of the game.

Reading

As you read, use the learning strategy *Use Selective Attention* (see page 66) to answer these questions: Why are Maria's friends worried about her? What do Maria's friends discover about her?

READ THIS!

The Artist

Samir, Carlos, Carmen, and Sophie were talking after school.

"I'm worried about Maria," Samir said. "I think she's sick because she's worried about the test in Mr. Gomez's class tomorrow."

Carmen said, "Maybe we should go and see her. We could try to talk to her about the test."

"Good idea," said Carlos. "You go ahead to Maria's. I'll meet you there."

Carmen, Samir, and Sophie went to see Maria.

"Maria, we're worried about you. Are you okay?" asked Carmen.

"No, I'm sick. But I should be better the day after tomorrow."

"The day *after* tomorrow? You can't miss the English test," said Carmen.

"Maria, are you worried about Mr. Gomez's test?" asked Sophie.

"Yes, I'm very worried about it."

"Maybe you're sick because you're worried about it," said Samir.

"I don't know," said Maria. "I mean . . . I *could* be sick because of the test."

"You shouldn't worry," said Carmen. "I'm sure you'll do well on the test."

"Really?" asked Maria. "Why are you so sure?"

"Because you studied for it," answered Carmen.

"And because you work hard and you're smart," added Samir.

"Hey, everyone," interrupted Sophie. "Look at this."

Sophie was pointing at a painting on the wall.

"This has Maria's name on it. Did you paint this picture, Maria?"

"Oh . . . yeah . . . I painted all the pictures in here," said Maria.

Everyone was surprised. They had no idea that Maria was an artist.

"You're a really good artist," said Samir. "Why didn't you tell us?"

"I don't know . . . I . . ."

Everyone started talking about Maria's beautiful paintings. Soon, they were all laughing and having fun.

There was a knock at the door. It was Carlos.

"These flowers are for you, Maria," said Carlos. "Please feel better."

Maria said, "Oh, Carlos, thank you. You know what? I feel a lot better now. I *am* going to take the test tomorrow! You're really great friends!"

AFTER YOU READ

A. Did you use the learning strategy *Use Selective Attention* to find the answers to the questions in *Before You Read*? Find the sentences in the story that answer each question. Discuss your answers with a classmate.

B. Create an exercise.

   1. Work with a classmate. Write five sentences about the reading in your notebook. Write three true sentences and two false sentences.

   2. Exchange your sentences with another pair of students. Read their sentences. Write *True* or *False* after the sentences.

   Check your work. How many of your answers are correct? Write the number of correct answers in your notebook.

Writing

A. You are going to give advice to someone. First, read the letters below.

> Dear Andrea,
>
> I have an important baseball game next Friday. The problem is I don't feel well. Every morning I have a headache, and every night I have a stomachache. What should I do?
>
> Sincerely,
> Tim

> Dear Tim,
>
> Relax! I don't think you're sick. I think you're nervous because of the game. You should get some rest and think about having fun on Friday.
>
> Yours truly,
> Andrea

B. Read the *Before I Write* checklist. In your notebook, write about a problem and how it could be solved.

WRITE THIS!

Read the *While I Write* checklist. Look at your notes and write a letter to an advice columnist. Then write the columnist's reply. Ask your teacher for new words.

AFTER YOU WRITE

A. Read the *After I Write* checklist. Then check your work.

B. Read your letters to a classmate. Listen to your classmate read his or her letters.

C. Write a final copy of your letters in your notebook.

Tools for Writing

Before I Write

▶ Study the models.

▶ Think about a problem I have or someone else might have.

▶ Make notes about . . .
   possible causes
   possible solutions

While I Write

▶ Start your letters with "Dear _____"

▶ Use **should** with a verb to state necessity or obligation.
   You should get some rest.

▶ Use **because** to tell why or give a reason.
   I think you're nervous because of the game.

▶ End your letters with "Sincerely" or "Yours truly"

After I Write

▶ Did I start my letters with "Dear _____"?

▶ Did I use *should* with a verb to state necessity or obligation?

▶ Did I use *because* to tell why or give a reason?

▶ Did I end my letters with "Sincerely" or "Yours truly"?

Learning Log

◆ VOCABULARY

Read the words and expressions. Then copy them into your notebook.
Underline the words and expressions you need to review.

Nouns				Expressions
Illnesses	**People**	**Other**		a couple of (days)
headache	artist	flower	office	By the way, . . .
sore throat	doctor	knock	plenty	Feel better.
stomachache	nurse	medicine		have (had) no idea
				the day after
Verbs		**Adjectives**		tomorrow
interrupt		curious	surprised	
stay		smart	terrible	

◆ LANGUAGE and LEARNING STRATEGIES

Copy the checklist into your notebook. Check what you know. Review what you
need to know.

I can . . .

_____ read and understand the dialogue "At the Nurse's Office"

_____ ask and answer questions using *should* and *could*

_____ make sentences using *because* clauses

_____ read and use new words with the vowel sound /ou/ as in *out*

_____ use the learning strategy *Use Selective Attention* to find key ideas
before I read

_____ read and understand the story "The Artist"

_____ write letters asking for and giving advice

◆ SELF-EVALUATION QUESTIONS

Answer the questions in your notebook.

1. What is easy in Chapter 17? What is difficult in Chapter 17?
2. How can you learn the things that are difficult?

Chapter 18

It was too easy.

Look at the picture. What things can you name in English? Say the words. Talk about what is happening in the picture.

A. Listen to the dialogue. Then answer these questions: Did everyone *really* think the test was easy? How do you know?

B. Read the dialogue.

The Test

Mr. Gomez: My, my. Why all the gloomy faces? You people used to like English class.

Samir: We still like English class. We just don't like tests.

Mr. Gomez: Don't worry, everyone. I know you're ready.

Carlos: I'm glad somebody thinks so.

* * * * *

(The students take the test. After class, everyone talks about it.)

Maria: I think I missed a lot of questions on the test. It was too difficult.

Liliana: I know I missed a few in the vocabulary section. That part was hard.

Maria: How did you do on the test, Carmen?

Carmen: I don't know. I think maybe I did okay.

Pablo: Me, too. In fact, I did better than I expected.

Maria: I did *worse* than I expected!

Carmen: Yeah, there were one or two hard questions on the test.

Maria: *One* or *two*?

Mei: To tell you the truth, I thought the test was too easy.

Maria: What?

Carlos: Mei's right. It wasn't hard enough.

Maria: Carlos! You, too?

Carlos: Maria, we're just teasing you. Of course the test was hard.

Maria:	Oh! I can't believe you people! You're the worst! Anyway, I hope I passed.	
Samir:	Stop worrying. I'm sure you passed.	
Maria:	You're right, Samir. I should just relax and wait to see my grade.	
Samir:	Yes! Exactly!	
Maria:	But I wonder how I did on the comprehension questions . . .	
Everyone:	Maria!	

Pair and Group Work

A. Read the dialogue with a classmate.

B. Act out the dialogue in groups of eight.

VOCABULARY

Words		Expressions
gloomy	pass	My, my.
face	relax	In fact, . . .
expect	grade	To tell you the truth, . . .
tease	wonder	I can't believe you!
hope	comprehension	Exactly!

A. Read and say the vocabulary. Then write the vocabulary in your notebook.

B. Use word analysis to study the vocabulary (see pages 250-251, Steps 1–3).

C. Find the vocabulary in the dialogue. Read the sentences that use the vocabulary.

D. Choose five words from the word box. In your notebook, write a mini-dialogue using these words. Practice your dialogue with a classmate.

Grammar 1

Comparatives and Superlatives: Irregular Adjectives

The adjectives *good* and *bad* have irregular comparative and superlative forms.

Adjective	Comparative	Superlative
good	better than	the best
bad	worse than	the worst

A. Copy the sentences into your notebook. Then fill in the blanks with the comparative or superlative form of *good* or *bad*.

1. Big Burger's hamburgers are *the best*.
2. Big Burger's hamburgers are _____ Ricky's.
3. Ricky's hamburgers are _____ Burger Pit's.
4. Burger Pit's hamburgers are _____ Ricky's.
5. Burger Pit's hamburgers are _____.

B. Read the conversation. Then listen.

A: Let's go to Burger Pit.

B: No. Burger Pit's hamburgers are the worst in town.

A: How about Ricky's? Their hamburgers are better.

B: Ricky's hamburgers are okay. But Big Burger's hamburgers are the best!

C. Practice the conversation in Exercise B with a classmate. Then make new conversations with your own information.

Grammar 2

Too and *not enough*

> **To o** means more than necessary or desired.
>   EXAMPLE: The test was **too** easy.
>
> **Not enough** means less than necessary or desired.
>   EXAMPLE: The test was **not** hard **enough**.

Look at the pictures. Then copy the sentences into your notebook. Complete the sentences with *too* or *not enough*.

1. The table *is too dirty* . (dirty)
   The table *isn't clean enough* . (clean)

2. The plate _____ . (small)
   The plate _____ . (big)

3. The coffee _____ . (hot)
   The coffee _____ . (cool)

4. The children _____ . (tall)
   The children _____ . (short)

Word Study

Other Vowel Sound: /ûr/

The letters *ur*, *ir*, and *er* can stand for the vowel sound /ûr/ as in *hurt*, *first*, and *her*.

A. Use the learning strategy *Sound Out* (see page 32) and the pictures to read the words.

1. Thursday

2. purple

3. nurse

4. bird

5. shirt

6. letter

7. mother

8. winter

B. Read the sentences aloud. Then copy them into your notebook. Circle the letters that stand for the vowel sound /ûr/.

1. I got a letter from my best friend yesterday.

2. Are they going to go to the library on Thursday?

3. My mother is cooking dinner right now.

4. Bic wants to buy a blue shirt at the mall.

5. Does she want to see the school nurse?

6. How much is that purple hat?

C. Look at Exercise A. Choose two words with the vowel sound /ûr/. In your notebook, write a sentence for each word.

Grammar 3

Statements with *used to*

Affirmative Statements			Negative Statements		
I, You, He/She, We, You, They	**used to**	like class.	I, You, He/She, We, You, They	**didn't use to**	like class.
Remember: Use *used to* for things that were true in the past but that are not true in the present. The negative form of *used to* is *didn't use to*.					

Copy the sentences into your notebook. Then fill in the blanks with *used to* or *didn't use to*.

1. Carlos _used to_ live in a smaller city. (affirmative)
2. Samir _____ walk to school, but now he does. (negative)
3. Sophie _____ dance in festivals when she was younger. (affirmative)
4. Mei _____ eat more Chinese food when she lived in China. (affirmative)
5. Liliana _____ like hamburgers, but now she does. (negative)

Yes/No Questions with *used to*

Did	I you he/she we you they	**use to** like class?	Yes,	you I he/she you we they	did.	No,	you I he/she you we they	didn't.
Remember: Form *yes/no* questions with *did + use to*.								

A. Read the conversation. Then listen.

A: Did you use to watch TV a lot when you were little?

B: Yes, I did. I used to read comic books a lot, too.

A: So did I.

B. Practice the conversation in Exercise A with a classmate. Then make new conversations using your own information.

Reading

BEFORE YOU READ

Use the learning strategy *Make Predictions* (see page 56).

1. Look at the pictures and the title of the story.
2. Look for words you know in the story.
3. What do you think the story is about?
4. Make a prediction.
5. Tell your prediction to your classmates.

READ THIS!

THE LAST DAY

The students were walking to English class together. "Today we find out what our test grades are," Bic told his friends.

"Do you think we don't know that?" asked Carmen.

"Really!" said Carlos. "I was awake for an hour last night wondering about my grade."

"I'm sure you did fine, Carlos," said Liliana. "You said the test was too easy."

"I was just teasing Maria, remember?" replied Carlos.

Maria stopped outside of Mr. Gomez's door. "I'm not going in there . . . ," she said. "I'm not brave enough."

Carmen took Maria by the elbow and gave her a little push. "Come on, Maria. You can do it."

They entered the room and found a surprise. There was a party in Mr. Gomez's classroom!

"Congratulations, everyone!" said Mr. Gomez. "You all passed the test. You're all promoted!"

There was a very loud "hooray" in the classroom as Mr. Gomez passed back the tests to everyone.

Maria looked pale. "I can't believe it. I passed."

Liliana shook Maria's shoulder. "Come on, Maria. You should be happy! You did it!"

"I'm happy. I'm happy," said the stunned Maria. "I just can't believe it." Everyone moved to the food and drink tables.

"Hey, Maria," said Samir. "What do you think about your grade?"

"I'm really happy," answered Maria. "I was so nervous before the test. But I did better than I expected."

"You know, Maria, you used to be nervous about everything, all the time," said Samir. "I think you're more relaxed now."

"Yes, I guess I *am* more relaxed," said Maria. "And I used to miss my home and my friends in El Salvador. I still love my country, but now my home is here. And I think I have the best friends in the whole world . . . right here at Washington School . . . right here in this room!"

AFTER YOU READ

A. Think about the learning strategy. What predictions did you make about the story before you read it? Were your predictions correct? As you read the story, did you need to change your predictions? What information or clues did you use to make your predictions? Discuss your answers with a classmate.

B. Read the questions. Then write the answers in your notebook.

1. Why was Maria afraid to go into Mr. Gomez's classroom?
2. What did the students find in Mr. Gomez's classroom?
3. Who passed the final test?
4. Maria is different than she used to be. What's different about her?

Check your work. How many of your answers are correct? Write the number of correct answers in your notebook.

Writing

A. You are going to write a new story about one of the characters. First, read the story below.

> Samir
>
> Samir was worried. He did not know what to study in college. He did not know what to do with his life. Samir was very worried.
>
> One night Samir was babysitting his little brother Ali. Ali brought Samir a book. Samir said, "Let's read the book together." Samir read the story to Ali. He stopped and pointed to certain words. He helped Ali say the words. When they finished the story, Ali was smiling. He said, "Samir, you are a good teacher!"
>
> Samir thought about reading to Ali. He liked helping Ali read the story. Suddenly he knew what he wanted to do. He wanted to become a teacher!

B. Read the *Before I Write* checklist. In your notebook, make notes about one of the characters. Then make notes about a new story.

WRITE THIS!

Read the *While I Write* checklist. Look at your notes and write a story about one of the characters. Ask your teacher for new words.

AFTER YOU WRITE

A. Read the *After I Write* checklist. Then check your work.

B. Read your story to a classmate. Listen to your classmate read his or her story.

C. Write a final copy of your story in your notebook.

Tools for Writing

Before I Write

▶ Study the model.

▶ Choose a character to write about. What do I already know about this character? Make notes.

▶ Create a new story. Make notes about . . .

  who is in the story
  where it is set
  what it is about

While I Write

▶ Give the story a title.

▶ Give the story a clear beginning and end.

▶ Make the story interesting.

▶ Use adjectives to describe the characters.

▶ Pay attention to punctuation.

After I Write

▶ Did I give the story a title?

▶ Did I give the story a clear beginning and end?

▶ Did I make the story interesting?

▶ Did I use adjectives to describe the character?

▶ Did I pay attention to punctuation?

Learning Log

◆ VOCABULARY

Read the words and expressions. Then copy them into your notebook.
Underline the words and expressions you need to review.

Nouns				Expressions
Parts of the Body		**Other**		Congratulations.
elbow		comprehension		Exactly!
face		grade		I can't believe you!
shoulder		push		In fact, . . .
		world		To tell you the truth, . . .
Verbs			**Adjectives**	
expect	pass back	shake (shook)	brave	stunned
find out	promote	tease	gloomy	whole
hope	relax	wonder	pale	
pass	reply			

◆ LANGUAGE and LEARNING STRATEGIES

Copy the checklist into your notebook. Check what you know. Review what you
need to know.

I can . . .

_____ read and understand the dialogue "The Test"

_____ compare two or three people or things using irregular adjectives

_____ use the expressions *too . . .* and *not . . . enough* correctly

_____ ask and answer questions using *used to* and *didn't use to*

_____ read and use new words with the vowel sound /ûr/ as in *hurt*

_____ use the learning strategy *Make Predictions* to guess what a story
will be about

_____ read and understand the story "The Last Day"

_____ write a story about one of the characters

◆ SELF-EVALUATION QUESTIONS

Answer the questions in your notebook.

1. What is easy in Chapter 18? What is difficult in Chapter 18?
2. How can you learn the things that are difficult?

Los Angeles

Chicago •

New York
City

FOCUS ON CONTENT

■ Life Science How Nature Works:
Ecosystems and Food Chains 210

■ Physical Science The Universe:
Earth and the Milky Way 212

■ Math Solving Word Problems:
Mathematics in Everyday Life 214

■ Literature Poetry:
Understanding Images 216

■ Social Studies The United States:
Reading Maps of Our Country 218

■ History Martin Luther King Jr.:
An American Hero 220

VOCABULARY HANDBOOK 222

GRAMMAR HANDBOOK 234

WORD ANALYSIS 250

THE WRITING PROCESS 252

USING A DICTIONARY 256

LEARNING STRATEGIES 258

GLOSSARY 259

INDEX 261

Apply what you learned in Unit 1 to the kinds of readings you will find in your classes. In Unit 1, you learned how to preview a reading. You talked about the pictures before you started to read. Look at the pictures in this reading. What things can you name in English? Previewing the pictures helps you to get ready to read.

How Nature Works
ECOSYSTEMS AND FOOD CHAINS

Ecosystems are all around us. They are how nature works. Every place on Earth—every forest, mountain, and ocean—has an ecosystem. All living things, including humans, are part of an ecosystem.

Ecosystems

Ecosystems have both living and non-living things. Plants and animals are living things. Sunlight, air, rocks, and soil are non-living things.

The living things in an ecosystem need both non-living things and other living things. For example, plants need soil, water, and sunlight. Animals need air, water, and food. Animals' food can be plants, other animals, or both.

This ecosystem has an animal (a chipmunk), a non-living thing (a piece of wood), and a plant. ▶

BEFORE YOU GO ON . . .

Give examples for each: a living thing and a non-living thing.

Food Chains

Plants, the animals that eat them, and the animals that eat those animals are all part of a food chain. In a food chain, each living thing is linked to the other living things in the chain. For example, a food chain can begin with a plant. The plant grows leaves. Then, a rabbit eats some of the leaves. Next, a fox eats the rabbit.

Rabbits need plants to live. Foxes need smaller animals to live. Every part of the food chain is important in an ecosystem.

▲ Food chain of a plant, a rabbit, and a fox

VOCABULARY

Look at the reading again. Write words you don't know in your notebook. Try to guess their meanings from other words around them. Then check a dictionary.

Science Words
ecosystem
food chain
living thing
non-living thing

COMPREHENSION

Read the questions and write the answers in your notebook.

1. Where are ecosystems?
2. What do ecosystems have?
3. What do animals need?
4. In a food chain, what is each living thing linked to?
5. Are you part of the food chain?

Apply what you learned in Unit 2 to the kinds of readings you will find in your classes. Use the learning strategy Make Predictions (see page 56) to try to guess what the reading is about. Look at the title, the headings, and the pictures. Then, look for words you know in the reading. What do you think the reading is about? Make a prediction, and tell your prediction to a classmate.

THE UNIVERSE
Earth and the Milky Way

How large is the universe? The universe has billions of galaxies, and each galaxy has billions of stars. Our Earth is one small planet in this galaxy of stars.

The Stars

From Earth, stars look like small lights in the night sky. But each star is really a giant ball of hot gas. Many stars are in small groups. The Big Dipper is a famous example of a group of stars.

Our sun is a medium-size star. Its core, or center, is very hot. The heat in the core of the sun reaches up to 15 million degrees centigrade (27 million degrees Fahrenheit)!

▲ The Big Dipper

BEFORE YOU GO ON . . .

What is the sun?

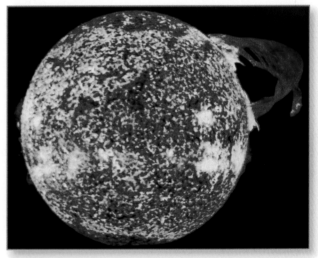

▲ The heat in the sun's core reaches up to 15,000,000° C (27,000,000° F).

The Solar System

Our sun is at the center of a solar system. In a solar system, planets go around a sun.

Nine planets go around our sun: Mercury, Venus, Earth, Mars, Jupiter, Saturn, Uranus, Neptune, and Pluto.

The Galaxy

Our solar system is part of the Milky Way galaxy. A galaxy is a very large group of stars. How large? There are about 200 billion (200,000,000,000) stars in the Milky Way galaxy! And the Milky Way is just one of billions of other galaxies in the universe.

▲ The planets of our solar system

VOCABULARY

Look at the reading again. Write words you don't know in your notebook. Try to guess their meanings from other words around them. Then check a dictionary.

Science Words
galaxy
Milky Way
planet
solar system
universe

COMPREHENSION

Read the questions and write the answers in your notebook.

1. What is a star?
2. How hot is the sun's core?
3. What is a galaxy?
4. How many stars are in our Milky Way?
5. Which is bigger, our solar system or our galaxy?

FOCUS ON CONTENT

History readings often include a lot of details. How can you remember the most important details? Here is a good learning strategy for doing this. Read the article carefully and take notes while you are reading. Write the important dates and events in your notebook. This will help you remember the order of events.

MARTIN LUTHER KING JR.
AN AMERICAN HERO

Martin Luther King Jr. was an American hero. His dream was for all people to have equal rights. He fought for that dream and helped to make it happen.

King's Early Life

Martin Luther King Jr. was born on January 15, 1929, in Atlanta, Georgia. At that time, African Americans were segregated from Caucasians in some states. They had to go to separate schools, and they had to eat at separate restaurants. They also had to sit at the back of buses.

Martin Luther King Jr. was a very good student. At fifteen, he finished high school. He went on to study at several colleges and universities. When he recieved his Ph.D he became "Doctor King".

▲ Martin Luther King Jr.

▲ An example of segregation in southern states

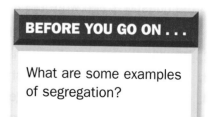

BEFORE YOU GO ON . . .

What are some examples of segregation?

Dr. King, Civil Rights Leader

In 1954, Dr. King joined other people who were fighting for equal rights for all Americans. The fight they led became known as the Civil Rights movement.

By 1962, Dr. King was the leader of the Civil Rights movement. In 1963, there was a large demonstration in Washington, D.C. More than 250,000 people came to the demonstration. Dr. King gave his most famous speech there, called *I Have a Dream.* The next year, one of Dr. King's dreams came true. Congress passed a law called the Civil Rights Act. This law made it illegal to discriminate against people because of their color, religion, or the country they came from.

On April 4, 1968, Dr. King was assassinated in Memphis, Tennessee. People all over the world were shocked and saddened by the death of this American hero. His courage and leadership helped millions of people and changed the United States forever.

▲ The Civil Rights protest in Washington, D.C.

VOCABULARY

Look at the reading again. Write words you don't know in your notebook. Try to guess their meanings from other words around them. Then check a dictionary.

History Words
assassinate
Civil Rights
  movement
demonstration
discriminate
equal rights
illegal
segregate

COMPREHENSION

Read the questions and write the answers in your notebook.

1. When was Dr. King born?
2. What were people in the Civil Rights movement fighting for?
3. What did Dr. King do in 1963?
4. What did the Civil Rights Act make illegal?
5. Do you think Dr. King was a hero? Why or why not?

Vocabulary Handbook—

1. listen to music

2. watch TV

3. read

4. play sports

5. ride my bike

6. go swimming

7. play my guitar

8. talk on the phone

9. play computer games

10. see friends

11. go shopping

12. go to the movies

A: What do you do in your free time?
B: I listen to music.
A: What else?
B: I play my guitar.

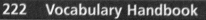

1. tall man   **2.** short man   **3.** big animal   **4.** small animal

5. clean shirt   **6.** dirty shirt   **7.** young person   **8.** old person

9. easy problem   **10.** hard problem   **11.** expensive ring   **12.** cheap ring

A: Point to the tall man.
B: He's this one.

1. red circle/ circular shape

2. yellow square/ square shape

3. blue rectangle/ rectangular shape

4. green triangle/ triangular shape

5. purple star/ star-like shape

6. orange oval/ oval shape

7. pink diamond/ diamond-like shape

8. gray tube/ tubular shape

9. black

10. white

11. brown

12. beige

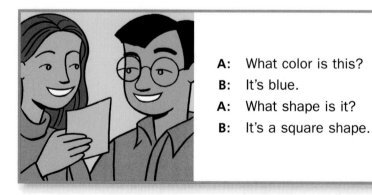

A: What color is this?
B: It's blue.
A: What shape is it?
B: It's a square shape.

1. a shirt

2. a belt

3. pants

4. socks

5. shoes

6. a skirt

7. a dress

8. shorts

9. a jacket

10. sneakers

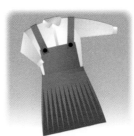

11. a uniform

12. a coat

A: What's Carlos wearing?
B: He's wearing a shirt, pants, and a belt.

1. chicken

2. beef

3. pork

4. fish

5. eggs

6. cheese

7. vegetables

8. fruit

9. rice

10. bread

11. cereal

12. dessert

A: What did you eat for dinner yesterday?

B: I ate chicken and rice.

1. get up

2. eat breakfast

3. take a shower

4. leave home

5. get to school

6. eat lunch

7. leave school

8. get home

9. eat dinner

10. do homework

11. watch TV

12. go to bed

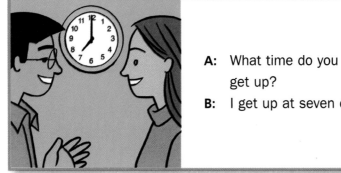

A: What time do you get up?
B: I get up at seven o'clock.

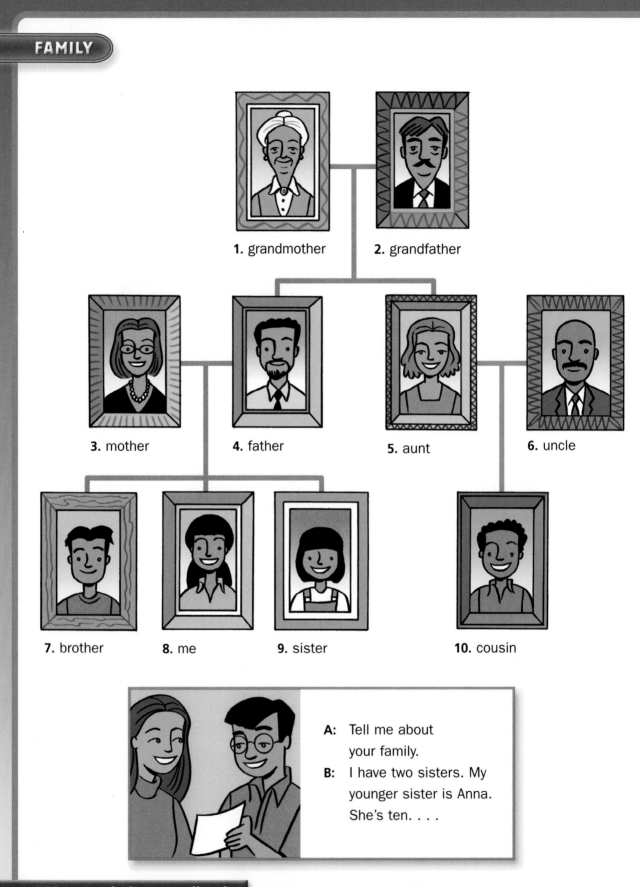

1. grandmother
2. grandfather
3. mother
4. father
5. aunt
6. uncle
7. brother
8. me
9. sister
10. cousin

A: Tell me about your family.
B: I have two sisters. My younger sister is Anna. She's ten. . . .

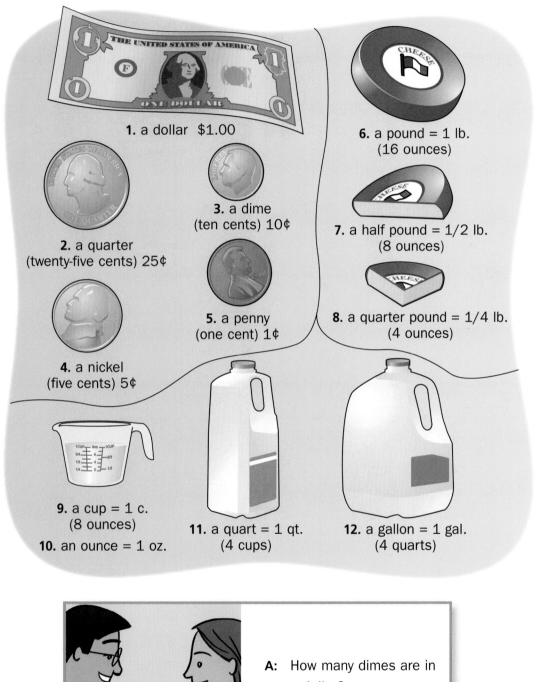

1. a dollar $1.00

2. a quarter
(twenty-five cents) 25¢

3. a dime
(ten cents) 10¢

4. a nickel
(five cents) 5¢

5. a penny
(one cent) 1¢

6. a pound = 1 lb.
(16 ounces)

7. a half pound = 1/2 lb.
(8 ounces)

8. a quarter pound = 1/4 lb.
(4 ounces)

9. a cup = 1 c.
(8 ounces)

10. an ounce = 1 oz.

11. a quart = 1 qt.
(4 cups)

12. a gallon = 1 gal.
(4 quarts)

A: How many dimes are in
a dollar?

B: Ten.

1. main entrance   **2.** hall   **3.** classroom   **4.** office

5. restroom   **6.** library   **7.** cafeteria   **8.** auditorium

9. science lab   **10.** gym   **11.** track   **12.** field

A: Where's the library?
B: It's next to the cafeteria.

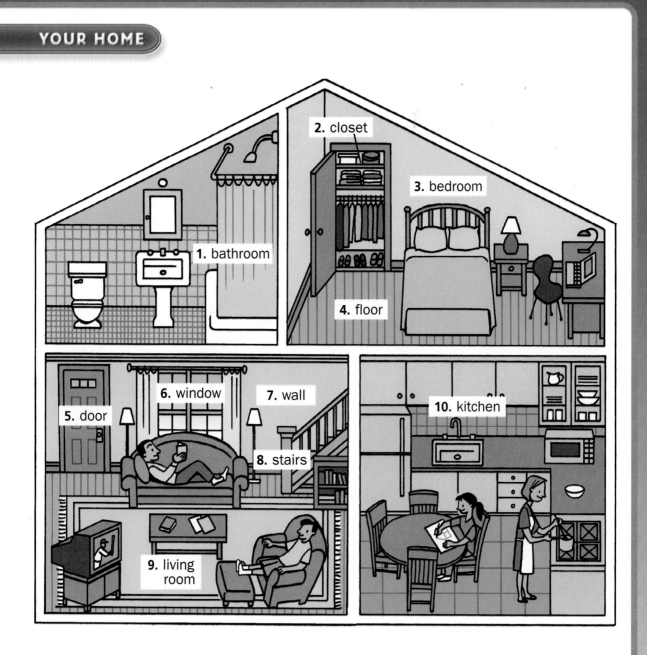

1. bathroom
2. closet
3. bedroom
4. floor
5. door
6. window
7. wall
8. stairs
9. living room
10. kitchen

A: What's your home like?

B: We have a living room and two bedrooms.

A: What color is your living room?

B: It's beige.

1. history

2. science

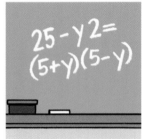

3. physical education (P. E.)

4. math

5. art

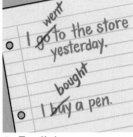

6. English

7. social studies

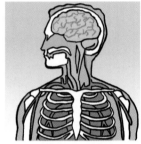

8. health

9. band

10. chorus

11. languages

12. computer science

A: What subjects do you like?
B: I like English and math.
A: Do you like history?
B: Not really.

Seasons

1. winter **2.** spring **3.** summer **4.** fall

Temperatures

5. hot **6.** warm **7.** cool **8.** cold

Weather Conditions

9. sunny **10.** cloudy **11.** rainy **12.** snowy

A: Where are you from?
B: I'm from Thailand.
A: What's Thailand like in the spring?
B: It's hot and sunny.

Grammar Handbook

English has eight **parts of speech**. Every English word belongs to one of these categories: noun, pronoun, adjective, verb, adverb, preposition, conjunction, or interjection.

Nouns

Nouns name people, places, or things.

Plural Nouns (page 33)

- A noun that names one thing is **singular**.
    turtle
    map
    boy

- A noun that names more than one thing is **plural**. Add **–s** to make most nouns plural.
    two turtle**s**
    five map**s**
    three boy**s**

- Some plural nouns follow special spelling rules:

    If a noun ends in s, x, sh, or ch, add **–es** to make it plural.
    bus ⟶ bus**es**   dish ⟶ dish**es**
    box ⟶ box**es**   lunch ⟶ lunch**es**

    If a noun ends in a consonant plus y, change the y to **i** and add **–es** to make it plural.
    baby ⟶ bab**ies**
    country ⟶ countr**ies**

    Some nouns have irregular plural forms.
    man ⟶ men   child ⟶ children
    woman ⟶ women   foot ⟶ feet

Count and Non-Count Nouns (page 126)

- Most nouns are things that can be counted. We call them **count nouns**. They can be singular or plural.
    a cookie   three cookies
    a student   nine students

- Some nouns stand for things that can't be counted. We call them **non-count nouns**.
    - lemonade
    - bread
- Non-count nouns have no plural form, but they can be "counted" in phrases like this:
    - a glass of lemonade   two glasses of lemonade
    - a slice of bread   six slices of bread

Possessive of Singular and Plural Nouns (page 43)

- A **possessive noun** tells who something belongs to. Add **'s** to form the possessive of a singular noun.
    - The girl**'s** book is on the floor.
- Add just an apostrophe (') to form the possessive of a plural noun that ends in **s**.
    - The girl**s'** books are on the floor.

Pronouns

Pronouns are words that take the place of nouns or proper nouns. In this example, the pronoun *she* replaces, or refers to, the proper noun *Maria*.

   proper noun   pronoun
Maria is not home. **She** is baby-sitting.

Subject Pronouns (page 20)

- Use a **subject pronoun** to replace a noun in subject position (in front of the verb).
    - **The student** is from Mexico. ⟶ **She** is from Mexico.
- The subject pronouns are *I*, *you* (singular), *he*, *she*, *it*, *we*, *you* (plural), and *they*.

Object Pronouns (page 87)

- Use an **object pronoun** to replace a noun in object position (after the verb).
    - Grandma is helping **Carlos**. ⟶ Grandma is helping *him*.
- The object pronouns are *me*, *you* (singular), *him*, *her*, *it*, *us*, *you* (plural), and *them*.

Possessive Pronouns (page 161)

- A **possessive pronoun** replaces a possessive adjective and a noun. It may be the subject or the object of a sentence.
    > This isn't *my backpack*. **Mine** is blue.
    > That's *your money*. It's **yours**.

my + noun	=	**mine**	*our* + noun	=	**ours**
your + noun	=	**yours**	*your* + noun	=	**yours**
his + noun	=	**his**	*their* + noun	=	**theirs**
her + noun	=	**hers**			
its + noun	=	**[no possessive pronoun]**			

Demonstrative Pronouns: *this, that, these, those* (pages 40–41)

- Use *this* to talk about a singular noun that is near you.
    > **This** is a folder.
- Use *that* to talk about a singular noun that is far from you.
    > **That** is a notebook.
- Use *these* to talk about a plural noun that is near you.
    > **These** are pens.
- Use *those* to talk about a plural noun that is far from you.
    > **Those** are pencils.

this

that

these

those

Adjectives

Adjectives describe nouns. An adjective usually comes before the noun it describes.
> **tall** boy
> **big** lunch
> **two** caps

An adjective can come after the noun it describes. This often happens in sentences with the verb *be*.
> Her book bag is **new**.
> His shirt was **dirty**.
> The tables were **green**.

Do not add –s to adjectives that describe plural nouns.

> the **red** books
> the **same** classes
> the **new** students

Possessive Adjectives (page 33)

- A **possessive adjective** comes before a noun. It tells who the noun belongs to.
  I have a pet. **My** pet is a turtle. **Its** name is Skipper.

I ⟶	**my**		we ⟶	**our**
you ⟶	**your**		you ⟶	**your**
he ⟶	**his**		they ⟶	**their**
she ⟶	**her**			
it ⟶	**its**			

Articles: *a* and *an* (page 40)

- **Articles** are a special kind of adjective. ***A*** and ***an*** are indefinite articles.
  They come before singular nouns.
  Mei has **a** pencil.
  She doesn't have **an** eraser.

- If there is another adjective before the noun, put ***a*** or ***an*** before the adjective.
  Carlos has **a** big backpack.

- Use ***a*** before nouns or adjectives that begin with consonant sounds. Use ***an***
  before nouns or adjectives that begin with vowel sounds.

a book	**an** English book
an apple	**a** red apple

Quantifiers: *some* and *any* (page 127)

- **Quantifiers** are another special kind of adjective. ***Some*** and ***any*** are quantifiers.
  In an affirmative statement, use ***some*** before a plural noun or a non-count
  noun to mean "a little" or "a few."
  Maria and her mother need **some** apples. They need **some** lettuce, too.

- In a negative statement, use ***any***.
  They don't need **any** potatoes. They don't need **any** coffee, either.

- Use *any* in *yes/no* questions. Place it before a plural noun or a non-count noun.
  Do you want **any** crackers?
  Do you want **any** milk?

Comparative Adjectives (page 136)

- **Comparative adjectives** compare two people, places, or things. Use the word *than* after a comparative adjective.

  Mei is **taller than** Sophie.

- To form the comparative of most short adjectives, add **–er**.

  old + **er** = **older**

- Some comparative adjectives follow special spelling rules:

  If an adjective ends in silent *e*, just add **–r** to make it comparative.

  late + **r** = **later**

  If an adjective ends in a consonant + *y*, change the *y* to *i* before adding *–er*.

  eas~~y~~ + **i** + **er** = **easier**

  If a one-syllable adjective ends in a consonant-vowel-consonant (CVC) pattern, double the last consonant before adding *–er*.

  big + **g** + **er** = **bigger**

Superlative Adjectives (page 137)

- **Superlative adjectives** compare three or more people, places, or things. Use the word *the* before a superlative adjective.

  Pablo is **the tallest** boy in the class. Samir is **the shortest**.

- To form the superlative of most short adjectives, add **–est**.

  old + **est** = **oldest**

- Some superlative adjectives follow special spelling rules:

  If an adjective ends in silent *e*, just add **–st** to make it superlative.

  late + **st** = **latest**

  If an adjective ends in a consonant + *y*, change the *y* to *i* before adding *–est*.

  eas~~y~~ + **i** + **est** = **easiest**

  If a one-syllable adjective ends in a consonant-vowel-consonant (CVC) pattern, double the last consonant before adding *–est*.

  big + **g** + **est** = **biggest**

Comparatives and Superlatives with *more* and *most* (page 139)

- Use *more* to form the comparative of adjectives with three or more syllables. Do not add *–er*.

  This book is **more expensive than** that book.

- Use *most* to form the superlative of adjectives with three or more syllables. Do not add *–est*.

  This book is **the most expensive** of all.

Comparatives and Superlatives: Irregular Adjectives (page 200)

- The adjectives *good* and *bad* have irregular comparative and superlative forms.

- Comparative adjectives compare two people, places, or things. Remember to use *than* after a comparative adjective.

    Ricky's hamburgers are **better than** Burger Pit's.

- Superlative adjectives compare three or more people, places, or things. Remember to use *the* before a superlative adjective.

    Burger Pit's hamburgers are **the worst** in town.

Adjective	Comparative	Superlative
good	better	best
bad	worse	worst

Verbs

Verbs express an action or a state of being.

subject verb
Samir **walks** to school.

- An **action verb** tells what someone or something does. You cannot always see the action of an action verb.

    Action verb
    Carmen **knows** the answer.

- A **linking verb** shows no action. It links the subject with another word that describes the subject. In this sentence, the noun *friend* tells something about the subject, *brother*. The linking verb is *is*.

    linking verb
    Your brother **is** my friend.

- A **helping verb** comes before the main verb. It adds to the main verb's meaning. Helping verbs can be forms of the verb *be*, *do*, or *have*.

    helping action
    verb verb
    I **am walking** to my English class.

    helping action
    verb verb
    He **has finished** the test.

- In a question, the subject comes between a helping verb and a main verb.

    helping action
    verb verb
    Did Liliana **give** Sophie the CD?

- Verbs take different forms to agree with their subjects.

    singular singular
    subject   verb
    Carlos **needs** a pencil.

         plural subject   plural verb
    Bic and Carlos **need** paper.

- The tense of a verb shows the time of an action or state of being.

         present tense
    Maria **studies** English every day.

              past tense
    Yesterday Maria **studied** history, too.

Present Tense of *be* (pages 21, 23, 53, 62, 116)

- Use the **present tense** to give facts and tell about things that happen regularly. The verb *be* has three present-tense forms: *am*, *is*, and *are*.

I	**am**	from El Salvador.	We	**are**	from El Salvador.
You	**are**		You		
He/She It	**is**		They		

- To make a negative statement, add *not* after the verb.
    Mr. Gomez **is not** from El Salvador.
- To make an information question, place the verb directly after the question word.
    Where is my backpack?
- To make a *yes/no* question, place the verb before the subject.
    He is a teacher. ⟶ **Is he** a teacher?
- There are two patterns for negative short answers with the present tense of *be*. Both patterns use contractions.
    No, **he's not**.   No, **he isn't**.
    No, **they're not**.   No, **they aren't**.

Present Tense of *have* (pages 30–31)

- The verb *have* has two present-tense forms: *have* and *has*.

I You	**have**	a brother.	We You They	**have**	a brother.
He/She It	**has**				

- To make a negative statement, use *do not have* or *does not have*. Do not use *has* in a negative statement. Use contractions in speaking and informal writing.

    You **do not have** math now.   You **don't have** math now.

    She **does not have** seven classes.   She **doesn't have** seven classes.

Present Tense of Regular Verbs (pages 63, 117)

- A regular verb has two forms in the present tense.

I You	**like**	music.	We You They	**like**	music.
He/She It	**likes**				

- To make a negative statement, use *do not* or *does not* before the base form of the verb. Use contractions in speaking and informal writing.

    I **do not speak** Spanish.   I **don't speak** Spanish.

    He **does not need** a map.   He **doesn't need** a map.

- To make an information question with a verb other than *be*, use *do* or *does* and the base form of the verb. Put the subject between the two parts of the verb.

    What **do** you **want**?

    Do not use *do* or *does* with information questions when the question is about the subject.

    subject
    Carlos likes popcorn. ⟶ Who likes popcorn?

- In formal speaking and writing, use **whom** to ask questions about an object. In informal speaking and writing, use **who**.

    Whom do they want to visit? (formal)

    Who do they want to visit? (informal)

- Sometimes we place a noun after the word *what* in a question. The noun tells what kind of answer we expect.

    What time do you come to school?

    I come to school **at 7:30**.

- To make a *yes/no* question with a verb other than *be*, add *do* or *does* before the subject. Always use the base form of the main verb.

    Does she like school?

    Do they speak English?

    Use *do, does, don't,* or *doesn't* in your short answer.

    Yes, she **does**.   No, she **doesn't**.

    Yes, they **do**.   No, they **don't**.

Present Continuous Tense (pages 84–85)

- Use the **present continuous tense** to tell about something that is happening right now. To form the present continuous, use the present tense of *be* and the base form of the verb + **-ing**. Use contractions in speaking and informal writing.

    I **am reading** a book.   **I'm reading** a book.

- To make a negative statement, add *not* between the form of *be* and the *-ing* verb. Use contractions in speaking and informal writing.

    She **is not washing** her hair.   **She's not washing** her hair.

                                         or

                                       She isn't washing her hair.

- Some verbs have special spelling rules when adding *-ing*.

    If a verb ends in a silent *e*, drop the *e* before adding *–ing*.

        write ⟶ **writing**

    If a one-syllable verb ends in a consonant-vowel-consonant (CVC) pattern, double the last consonant before adding *-ing* (except when the final consonant is *w*, *x*, or *y*).

        get ⟶ **getting**

- To make an information question, place the subject between the two parts of the verb.

    Who **am** I **going** with?
    What **are** you **making**?

- To make a *yes/no* question, place the present-tense form of *be* (*am*, *is*, or *are*) before the subject.

    Is she studying?

- There are two patterns for negative short answers in the present continuous tense. Both patterns use contractions.

    No, **she's not**.   No, **she isn't**.
    No, **they're not**.   No, **they aren't**.

Past Tense of *be* (pages 75, 116)

- Use the **past tense** to tell about events that happened in the past and are completed. The verb *be* has two past-tense forms: *was* and *were*.

    Mei **was** in the gym.
    You **were** at school yesterday.

- To make a past-tense negative statement, add *not* after the verb. In speaking and informal writing, use contractions.

    Mei **was not** in the gym.   Mei **wasn't** in the gym.
    You **were not** at school yesterday.   You **weren't** at school yesterday.

- To make an information question, place the verb directly after the question word.
   When was the party?

- To make a *yes/no* question, place the verb before the subject.
   Was he late for class?
   Were they sick?

Past Tense of Regular and Irregular Verbs (pages 104–105, 107, 117)

- To make the past tense of most regular verbs, add **–ed** to the base form. The past tense form is the same for all persons.
   need ⟶ **needed**

- Some regular verbs have special spelling rules in the past tense:

   If a verb ends in a silent *e*, just add **–d**.
   dance ⟶ **danced**

   If a verb ends in a consonant + *y*, change the *y* to *i* before adding **–ed**.
   study ⟶ **studied**

- Many verbs have irregular forms in the past tense. We do not add *–ed* to make the past tense of these verbs.

break	⟶ **broke**		have	⟶ **had**
buy	⟶ **bought**		know	⟶ **knew**
come	⟶ **came**		light	⟶ **lit**
do	⟶ **did**		make	⟶ **made**
eat	⟶ **ate**		say	⟶ **said**
fall	⟶ **fell**		teach	⟶ **taught**
find	⟶ **found**		think	⟶ **thought**
go	⟶ **went**		write	⟶ **wrote**

- To make a negative statement, add *did not* before the base form of the verb. Do not use the *–ed* form or the irregular past-tense form.
   Carlos **did not make** the pizza.   Carlos **didn't make** the pizza.

- To make an information question with a verb other than *be*, use *did* and the base form of the verb. Put the subject between the two parts of the verb.
   What **did** she **find**?

   Remember, in formal speaking and writing, use *whom* to ask questions about an object.
   Whom did they see at the store? (formal)
   Who did they see at the store? (informal)

- To make a *yes/no* question with a verb other than *be*, add *did* before the subject. Always use the base form of the verb.
   Did Carlos **burn** the enchiladas?
   Did his friends **come** to the party?

   Use *did* or *didn't* in your short answer.
   Yes, he **did**.   No, he **didn't**.
   Yes, they **did**.   No, they **didn't**.

Past Tense with *used to* (page 203)

- Use *used to* plus the base form of a verb to talk about something that was true or often happened in the past but is not true or does not happen in the present.

    I **used to live** in a small town. Now I live in a big city.

- The negative form of *used to* is **didn't use to**. Use the negative form in speaking and informal writing, but avoid it in formal writing.

    I **didn't use to** like Japanese food, but now I do.

Past Continuous Tense (pages 158–159)

- Use the **past continuous tense** to tell about an action that was happening at a specific time in the past. To form the past continuous tense, use the past tense of *be* and the base form of the verb + *ing*.

    I **was writing** in my journal Saturday evening.

- To make a negative statement, add *not* between the form of *be* and the –*ing* verb. In speaking and informal writing, use the contractions *wasn't* and *weren't*.

    They **were not studying** last night.   I **wasn't studying** last night.

- Use the simple past tense and the past continuous tense in the same sentence to show that an event interrupted the continuing action in the past.

    I **was listening** to Ms. Kim when the lights **went** out.

Future Tense with *be going to* (pages 148–149)

- Use the **future tense with *be going to*** to talk about the immediate future, to make predictions, and to tell about plans that were made before now. Use a present-tense form of *be* plus *going to* and the base form of a verb. Use contractions in speaking and informal writing.

    She **is going to eat** lunch soon.   She's **going to eat** lunch soon.

- To make an information question, place the subject between a present-tense form of *be* and a verb phrase with *going to*.

    What **is** Sophie **going to do**?

    Use a future-tense statement with *be going to* to answer an information question. In speaking and informal writing, use contractions.

    She is going to go shopping.   **She's** going to go shopping.

- To make a *yes/no* question, place the present-tense form of *be* before the subject.

    Is he going to call his parents?

    Use a present-tense form of *be* in your short answer.

    Yes, he **is**.

- There are two patterns for negative short answers. Both patterns use contractions.

    No, **he's not**.   No, **he isn't**.

Future Tense with *will* (pages 168–169)

- Use the **future tense with *will*** to give general facts about the future, to make promises, and to tell about sudden ideas or decisions. Use *will* plus the base form of a verb. Use contractions in speaking and informal writing.

I **will invite** my grandmother.	I'**ll invite** my grandmother.
That **will help** Maria.	That'**ll help** Maria.

- To make a negative statement, use *will not*. In speaking and informal writing, use the contraction **won't**.

  The club **will not** meet tomorrow.   The club **won't** meet tomorrow.

- To ask an information question, place the subject between *will* and the base form of the verb.

  What **will** Maria **bring**?

  Sometimes we place a noun or noun phrase after the word *what* in a question.

  What **time** will the meeting start?

  If the question is about the subject, place *will* + the base form of the verb directly after the question word.

  Who **will study** together?

  Use a statement in the future tense with *will* to answer an information question. In speaking and informal writing, use contractions.

  What will Maria bring?   **She'll** bring homemade empanadas.

- To make a *yes/no* question, place *will* before the subject.

  Will they come to the meeting?

  Use *will* or *won't* in your short answer.

  Yes, they **will**.
  No, they **won't**.

Verbs + Infinitive (pages 95, 97)

- Some verbs, such as *like*, *want*, and *have*, can be followed by a noun.

  I **like tacos**.
  She **wants a new watch**.

- Some of these verbs can also be followed by the infinitive (the base form + *to*) of another verb:

  I **like to paint**.
  They **have to study**.

- To make a negative statement, add *do not* or *does not* before the correct form of *like*, *have*, or *want*. In speaking and informal writing, use the contractions *don't* and *doesn't*.

They **do not like** to baby-sit.	They **don't like** to baby-sit.
She **does not have** to work.	She **doesn't have** to work.

Verbs + Gerunds (page 183)

- Some verbs, such as *like*, *love*, and *enjoy* can be followed by a noun.

  Mei **loves Chinese food**.

  Some of these verbs can also be followed by gerunds. A gerund is a verb form that is used in place of a noun. To make a gerund, add **–ing** to the base form of a verb.

  Maria **enjoys painting**.

  These verbs can be followed by gerunds: *like*, *enjoy*, *love*, *hate*, *prefer*, *stop*, *start*, and *finish*.

Adverbs

Adverbs describe the action of verbs. They tell how an action happens. Adverbs answer the questions *Where? When? How? How much?* or *How often?* Many adverbs end in *–ly*.

       verb   adverb
They **walked** home **quickly**.

Adverbs of Frequency

- **Adverbs of frequency** tell how often we do something. Common adverbs of frequency include *always*, *often*, *rarely*, *usually*, *sometimes*, and *never*.

- Adverbs of frequency are often used with present-tense verbs. They come after the verb *be*.

  Carmen **is sometimes** late for class.

- Adverbs of frequency come before most other present-tense verbs.

  He **usually does** his homework after dinner.

Too and *not enough* (page 201)

- The adverb **too** means "more than necessary or desired." Use *too* before an adjective to express a negative idea.

  This table is **too small**.

- The adverb **enough** means "just the right amount." Use *enough* after an adjective to express a positive idea.

  This table is **big enough**.

- *Too* and *enough* have the opposite meanings in negative statements with *not*.

  This table is **not too small**.   (It's big enough.)
  This table is **not big enough**.   (It's too small.)

Prepositions

Prepositions are words that show time, place, or direction. Some common prepositions are *before*, *after*, *at*, and *to*.

> Carlos went **to** soccer practice **after** school.

Notice that a noun or pronoun usually follows a preposition. Together they form a **prepositional phrase**.

> I have math **after lunch**.
> Are you going **to the meeting**?

Prepositions of Location: *in, on, under, next to* (page 52)

- *In*, *on*, *under*, and *next to* are prepositions of location. They tell where something is.

> The book is **in** the backpack.

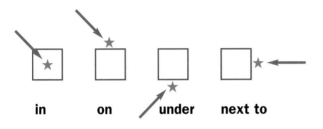

in	**on**	**under**	**next to**

Conjunctions

A **conjunction** is a word that joins two words, phrases, or whole sentences. Some common conjunctions are *and*, *but*, *or*, *for*, *nor*, *yet*, and *so*.

> We were at the party **for** three hours.
> They are at Ricky's **or** at the supermarket.

And, but, and so (page 129)

- The conjunctions *and*, *but*, and *so* connect two ideas. They can join two sentences to make a compound sentence. Use **and** to show that two ideas are similar.

> Sophie wants some coffee, **and** Mei wants some lemonade.

- Use **but** to show that two ideas are different. The second idea may be surprising.

> Sophie and Mei want some cookies, **but** Carmen doesn't want any.

- Use **so** to show that one idea comes from another idea.

> Mei is thirsty, **so** she wants some lemonade.

Interjections

Interjections are words or phrases that express emotion. Interjections that express strong emotion are followed by an exclamation point.

> **Wow!** Did you see that catch?
>
> **Hey!** Watch out for that ball!

Interjections that express mild emotion are followed by a comma.

> **Gee**, I'm sorry that your team lost.
>
> **Oh**, it's OK. We'll do better next time.

MODALS

Modals are used before the base form of a verb to change or add to the meaning of that verb. Modals express ideas such as possibility and ability.

Ability: *can* (page 65)

- Use **can** before a present-tense verb to talk about ability.
    Carlos and Carmen **can** speak Spanish.

- The negative form of **can** is **cannot**. In speaking and informal writing, use the contraction **can't**.
    They **can't** speak Chinese.

Possible Future: *may* and *might* (page 171)

- Use **may** or **might** before a present-tense verb to talk about possibility in the future. The two words have similar meanings, and in most sentences you can use either one. *May* expresses a slightly stronger possibility than *might* does.
    I **might** go to the movies tonight.   (It's possible.)
    I **may** go to the movies tonight.   (It's more possible.)

- Use **may not** or **might not** to express a negative possibility in the future.
    Maria **might not** study on Sunday.   (It's possible.)
    Maria **may not** study on Sunday.   (It's more possible.)

Advice: *should* (page 190)

- Use **should** to give advice or talk about what is right to do. Place **should** before the base form of a verb.
    They **should** study for the test.

- Use **should not** to make a negative statement. In speaking and informal writing, use the contraction **shouldn't**.
    He **should not** talk so much.   He **shouldn't** talk so much.

Suggestions: *could* (page 191)

- Use *could* to make a suggestion in an informal way. Place *could* before the base form of a verb. Statements with *could* are not as strong as statements with *should*.

    We **could** go to a movie.

CONTRACTIONS

A **contraction** is one word that replaces two words. Contractions are used in speaking and informal writing.

You are from the United States. ⟶ **You're** from the United States.

In a contraction, an apostrophe (') replaces the missing letters.

Contractions: Subject Pronouns and the Present Tense of *be* (page 21)

- When a present-tense form of *be* follows a subject pronoun, the following contractions are commonly used:

I am ⟶	**I'm**	we are ⟶	**we're**	
you are ⟶	**you're**	you are ⟶	**you're**	
he is ⟶	**he's**	they are ⟶	**they're**	
she is ⟶	**she's**			
it is ⟶	**it's**			

SENTENCE PATTERNS

There are four types of sentences: statements, questions, commands, and exclamations.

- A **statement** ends with a period.
    Maria is worried about the test.
- A **question** ends with a question mark.
    Why is Maria sick?
- A **command** may end with a period or an exclamation mark.
    Drink plenty of water.
    Don't touch that!
- An **exclamation** ends with an exclamation mark.
    We all passed the test!

Word Analysis

You can learn a lot about how to read, write, and say words in English by analyzing their letters and sounds. Follow these steps whenever you learn new vocabulary:

Step 1: RECOGNIZING LETTERS

1. Read the words in your notebook.
2. Work with a classmate. Take turns naming the letters in each word.

A: How do you spell brother?

B: B-R-O-T-H-E-R.

Step 2: FINDING SYLLABLES

> A **syllable** is a word part that has one vowel sound. A syllable may also have one or many consonant sounds. Here are examples of syllables:
>
> you   dol·lar   com·put·er   build·ing

1. Say each word out loud. Decide how many syllables you hear. For example:
   name   (1 syllable)
   brother   (2 syllables)
   umbrella   (3 syllables)
2. If a word has more than one syllable, draw lines to separate the syllables. For example:
   name
   bro/ther
   um/brel/la

Step 3: UNDERSTANDING PATTERNS

1. Look at each word. Circle any silent letters. For example:
   name
   brother   (no silent letters)
   umbrella   (no silent letters)

2. Look at each word. Underline any double letters. For example:

name   (no double letters)
brother   (no double letters)
umbre<u>ll</u>a

3. Study each word. Do any of its letters or letter combinations make unexpected sounds? Write about these sounds. Ask your teacher if you need help writing the new sounds. For example:

name   no unexpected sounds
brother   *t* and *h* can combine to make a new sound: /th/
umbrella   *a* can make the short vowel sound /u/

4. Work with a classmate. Take turns writing the words from memory.

Sounds and Their Spellings		
Sound	**Examples**	**Page**
short vowel sounds		
/a/	cap	32
/i/	pig	32
/o/	box	32
/e/	pen	42
/u/	sun	42
long vowel sounds		
/ā/	game, train, day	86, 96
/ē/	meat, tree, baby, me, field	106
/ī/	hi, cry, dime, pie, night	86, 118
/ō/	go, toe, stove, coat, window	86, 128
/yo͞o/	huge, music, few	86, 138
other vowel sounds		
/o͞o/	June, glue, new, moon	150
/o͝o/	hook	160
/ô/	author, straw	170
/oi/	coin, toy	182
/ou/	brown, mouse	192
/ûr/	nurse, bird, letter	202
consonant sounds		
/ch/	chin	54
/sh/	ship	54
consonant blends	clock, dress, flag, stop, swim	64
	gift, belt, lamp, hand, tent	74

The Writing Process

The **writing process** is a set of steps that writers follow. These steps will help you to express your ideas and share information in a clear and interesting way.

Step 1: PREWRITE

Before you begin to write, you must choose a **topic**.

Topic:	the subject you're going to write about
Examples:	*playing the guitar* *the latest Harry Potter book*
	a great soccer game *your favorite vacation*

If you need help choosing a topic, try **brainstorming**: Make a list of all the topic ideas you can think of. Write down everything! Then read your list. Which idea sounds the most interesting? Choose that idea for your topic.

You must also decide on the **purpose** and **audience** for your writing.

Purpose:	your reason for writing
Examples:	*to tell how to play the guitar*
	to give your opinion of a book you've read
	to report on a soccer game
	to describe what you did and saw on a vacation
Audience:	the person or people who will read your writing
Examples:	*your teacher* *your classmates*
	your family members *your friends*

Do you know enough to write about your topic? If you need more information, collect it now. Use the library or Internet, or talk to people who know about your topic.

Step 2: DRAFT

Imagine that you are talking to your audience. What do you want to say about your topic? Don't worry about grammar and spelling—just start writing. Include lots of details and examples to make your writing interesting. Keep writing until you've finished a **first draft**.

Step 3: REVISE

Read your first draft carefully. As you read, ask yourself questions like these:

- Is my main idea stated clearly?
- Are my ideas presented in the best order?
- Did I use specific details and examples?
- Does my draft have a beginning, middle, and end?

If your answer to any of the questions is *no*, make changes in your writing. Move paragraphs or sentences around. Add new words and sentences. Cross out words and sentences you don't want.

If possible, ask a classmate or family member to read your first draft. A reader's comments can help you decide what to change.

A student named Donna wrote a description of her trip to Arizona. Read Donna's first draft below.

>   Last August my family ~~went~~ *drove* to Arizona. We went to the grand canyon and sagwaro national park. We ~~went to~~ *visited* Tuscon too. we saw many interesting places. *I think everyone should visit Arizona especially if you like hot weather.*
>
>   First we went to the grand canyon. ~~The traffic was awful, but the canyon was wonderful.~~ It was so big. We rode into the canyon on mules. The ride was bumpy, *dusty and* but I was ~~happy~~ *excited* to be inside the canyon.
>
>   Next we went to Tuscon. Near Tuscon is sagwaro national park. It is full of cactus. *sagwaros and other kinds of* The whole area is a desert. It is very hot and dry.
>
>   Arizona is a ~~interesting~~ *amazing* state. It has ~~nice~~ *interesting* cities and beautiful *national* parks.

First, make a second draft of your paper, making all the changes you marked in Step 3. (If you're working on the computer, you will already have a clean second draft.) Now you're ready to **proofread** or check your work and make final corrections.

Read your second draft very slowly. Look for mistakes in grammar, spelling, punctuation, and style.

Correct every mistake you see. If you're working on paper, use a colored pen or pencil so you can see the corrections easily.

Look at how Donna corrected some of her mistakes:

> Last August my family drove to Arizona. We went to the grand canyon and sagwaro national park. We visited Tuscon, too. we saw many interesting places.

Prepare a final copy of your writing to **publish**, or share with your audience. First, recopy your writing, correcting the mistakes you marked in Step 4. (If you're working on the computer, you will already have a final copy.)

Next, think about how to make your writing look interesting. Donna made a poster about her vacation to show her friends. (See page 255.)

If you wrote a letter, you might copy it onto pretty stationery. If you wrote an essay about playing the guitar, you could add a title page and a picture of a guitar. Here are some other ideas for publishing your writing:

- Photocopy your final copy and give copies to your classmates.
- Post your writing on a secure website.
- Email your final copy to a friend.
- Send your writing to a school newspaper or magazine for possible publication.

My Trip

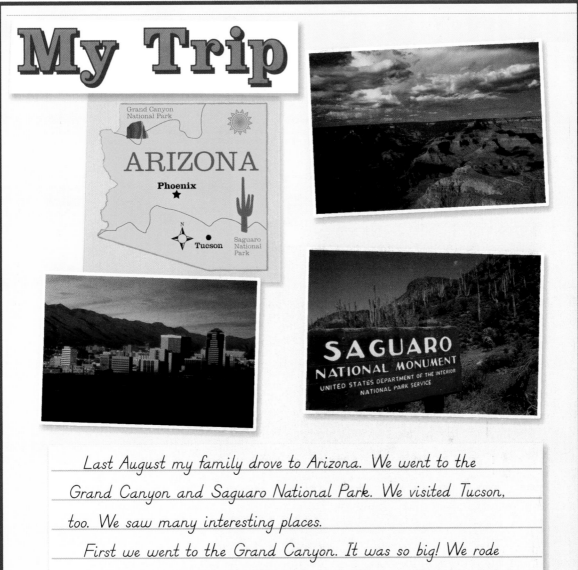

    Last August my family drove to Arizona. We went to the Grand Canyon and Saguaro National Park. We visited Tucson, too. We saw many interesting places.

    First we went to the Grand Canyon. It was so big! We rode into the canyon on mules. The ride was dusty and bumpy, but I was excited to be inside the canyon.

    Next we went to Tucson. Near Tucson is Saguaro National Park. It is full of saguaros and other kinds of cacti. The whole area is a desert. It is very hot and dry.

    Arizona is an amazing state. It has interesting cities and beautiful national parks. You should think about visiting Arizona, especially if you like hot weather!

Using a Dictionary

Dictionaries have helpful information about words. You can find the spelling, pronunciation, part of speech, and definitions of words. Most dictionaries have the following features. Look at the next page to see an example of each one.

Guide Words

At the top of each dictionary page is a guide word. It tells the first or last entry word on the page.

Entry Words

Entry words are printed in boldface type and are listed in alphabetical order.

Definitions

The definition tells you the meaning of a word. Many words have more than one definition. The definitions are numbered, with the most common one listed first.

Example Sentences

Example sentences show how to use an entry word.

Illustrations

Illustrations help show the meaning or meanings of an entry word.

Syllables

Each entry word is divided into syllables. Dots are used between the syllables.

Pronunciation

The pronunciation of an entry word is shown between slashes / /. The key to the pronunciation symbols appears at the front of the dictionary. The key tells what sounds the symbols represent.

Stress Mark

A stress mark /'/ before a syllable tells you to put more stress, or force, on that syllable.

Part of Speech

The dictionary shows the part of speech for each entry word. The part of speech tells how the word is used in a sentence. The eight parts of speech and their abbreviations are:

noun (n)	adverb (adv)	preposition (prep)
verb (v)	pronoun (pron)	interjection (interj)
adjective (adj)	conjunction (conj)	

guide word ———→ **famous**

entry word ———→ **fa•mous** /ˈfeɪməs/ *adj* known about or recognized by many people: *France is famous for its food and wine.*

definition ———→ **fan¹** /fæn/ *n* 1 someone who likes or admires a person, sport, type of music, etc.: *I'm not a fan of country music.* 2 a machine or device that moves the air to make people feel cooler

example sentence ———→

illustrations ———→

fan² *v* –nned, -nning to make air move around by waving something: *She fanned her face with a newspaper.*

syllables ———→ **fa•nat•ic** /fəˈnætɪk/ *n* someone who has extreme beliefs
pronunciation ———→ and behavior, especially in the areas of religion or politics

fan club *n* an organization for fans of a particular team, famous person, etc.

stressmark ———→ **fan•cy** /ˈfænsi/ *adj* 1 expensive and not simple or ordinary: *a fancy hotel* 2 having a lot of decorations: *I want some plain black shoes, nothing fancy.*

part of speech ———→ **fang** /fæŋ/ *n* a long, sharp tooth of an animal such as a snake or a dog

fan mail *n* letters sent to famous people by their fans

Learning Strategies

Strategy		Description
Make Inferences		Use information in a story to make good guesses about meaning.
Make Predictions		Try to guess what is going to happen next in a story. Use clues or information from the story to make predictions.
Personalize		Understand how a character feels, thinks, and acts by thinking about your own life (your experiences, knowledge, and feelings) and ways in which you are like the character.
Sound Out		Learn or discover rules about letter and sound relationships. Apply the rules to new words. Pay attention to patterns.
Use Selective Attention		Focus on key ideas and words to understand what you read.
Use What You Know		Think about and use what you already know about the topic of a story.

Glossary

BASE FORM
The base form is the simplest form of a verb. It has no added endings (such as -s, -ing, or -ed). Examples: *have*, *play*, *need*

CHECKLIST
A checklist is a list of things to do for a particular job or activity.

CONTRACTION
A contraction is a word made by putting two other words together. An apostrophe (') shows where a letter or letters have been left out. Contractions are common in speaking and informal writing. Examples: *I'm*, *doesn't*, *can't*

DIALOGUE
A dialogue is a conversation between two or more people.

EXPRESSION
An expression is a word, phrase, or sentence that has a special meaning. Examples: *Cool! How are you? You're welcome.*

INFINITIVE
The infinitive is the base form of a verb plus *to*. Examples: *to have*, *to play*, *to need*

INFORMATION QUESTION
An information question is a question that asks for information. Information questions start with *who*, *what*, *when*, *where*, *why*, or *how*.

INTERVIEW
To interview someone is to ask him or her questions for the purpose of collecting information.

JOURNAL
A journal is a written description of a person's activities, thoughts, or feelings. Some people write in a journal every day. The separate parts of a journal are called *entries*. Journal entries are usually personal and informal. A journal may be handwritten in a notebook or typed on a computer.

LEARNING STRATEGY
A learning strategy is a specific skill or plan used to learn or understand something. Examples: *Make Predictions*, *Sound Out*

LETTER
A letter is a written message from one person to another. Most letters have a greeting, a body, and a closing.

PARAGRAPH
A paragraph is a group of sentences about one main idea. The first line of a paragraph is usually indented (moved in toward the center of the page a little bit).

POEM
A poem is a piece of writing that expresses thoughts, feelings, or ideas. Poems are usually written in short, rhythmic lines. Many poems contain rhyming words (words that have the same ending sounds).

PUNCTUATION
Punctuation is a set of symbols that helps readers understand a piece of writing. Punctuation marks divide writing into phrases and sentences and give clues about their meaning. Examples: period (.), comma (,), question mark (?), exclamation point (!)

QUESTION WORD

Who, *what*, *when*, *where*, *why*, and *how* are question words. They mark the beginning of an information question.

SCRIPT

A script is the written form of a speech, play, movie, or other oral presentation. It tells what each person in the performance will say.

SENTENCE

A sentence is a group of words that expresses a complete thought. Every sentence has a subject and a verb. Statements, questions, and commands are types of sentences.

SONG

A song is a piece of music with words.

STATEMENT

A statement is a sentence that states a fact, opinion, or idea. Some statements are positive and others are negative. Examples: *I like lettuce. I don't like carrots.*

STORY

A story is a short piece of writing that has characters and a plot (action). It has a clear beginning, middle, and end. The purpose of most stories is to entertain the reader.

SYLLABLE

A syllable is a word part that has one vowel sound. A syllable may also have one or more consonant sounds.
Examples: *syl•la•ble*; *tel•e•phone*; *gui•tar*

WORD ANALYSIS

Word analysis is a way of studying (analyzing) the letters and sounds that make up a word. It is a useful strategy for learning and remembering new vocabulary and reading new words.

WRITING PROCESS

The writing process is a series of steps that help writers express ideas and share information in a clear and interesting way. The steps are *prewrite*, *draft*, *revise*, *edit*, and *publish*.

YES/NO QUESTION

A *yes/no* question is a question that must be answered with *yes* or *no*. It does not ask for new information.

Index

Numbers indicate chapters. GS = Getting Started; VH = Vocabulary Handbook

A

Acting out a dialogue, 1–2, 4–11, 13–18
Acting out a story, 1, 3, 11
Activities
 daily, 7, 16, VH
 free-time, 8, 13–16, 18, VH
 household, 7, 14
Adjectives
 comparative, 12, 18
 descriptive, 6, 10, VH
 possessive, 2, 14
 superlative, 12, 18
Adverbs of frequency, 16
Advice, giving and asking for, 17
Alphabet, GS, 1
Alphabetical order, 1
And, 11
Articles (*a*, *an*), 3

B

Baby-sitting, 5
Be, 1, 4–6, 10
Because clauses, 17
Birthdays, GS, 9
But, 11

C

Can (for ability), 5
Capital letters, 1–2, 5, 8
Clothes, 10, VH
Colors, VH
Commands, GS, 13
Comparisons, 2, 12, 18
Conjunctions, 11
Consonant sounds
 digraphs: /ch/, /sh/, 4
 final blends, 6
 initial blends, 5
Consonants, 1, 3, 12
Contractions
 can't, 5
 didn't, 9
 doesn't, *don't*, 5, 8
 how's, 10
 isn't, *aren't*, 7, 13
 shouldn't, 17
 subject pronouns and *be*, 1, 7
 subject pronouns and *will*, 15
 that's, 3
 there's, 4
 what's, 5, 7, 10
 wasn't, *weren't*, 6, 14
 where's, 4, 10
 who's, 10
 won't, 15
Could (for suggestions), 17
Countries, 1–2, 6, 15–16

D

Dates, GS, 9
Days of the week, GS, 6
Descriptions
 of people, 1, 8, 12, 15–16, 18
 of places, 4
 using *too* and *not enough*, 18
Directions, giving and asking for, 4–5
Do, 6, 10

E

Emergencies, 13–14
Expressions of frequency, 16

F

Families, 1, 7–8, 15, VH
Feelings, 5–6, 8, 12–13, 15–18
Filling out a form, 5
Foods, 11, VH
Friendship, 12–13, 17–18
Future tense
 with *going to*, 13
 with *will*, 15

G

Gerunds, 16
Greetings, 1–2

H

Have, 2
Have + infinitive, 8
Health, 13, 17
Help, asking for, 7, 13

I

Information questions
    in future tense with *going to*, 13
    in future tense with *will*, 15
    in past continuous tense, 14
    with *be*, 4, 5, 10
    with *do*, 6, 8, 10
Interviewing someone, 8, 16
Introductions, GS, 1, 9
Invitations, 5, 8
Irregular verbs, 9

J

Jobs, 5, 8, 11
Journal, 6

L

Languages, 1–2, 6, 15
Learning strategies
    make inferences, 9, 13
    make predictions, 4, 6–7, 10, 18
    personalize, 15
    use selective attention, 5, 11, 14, 17
    sound out, 2–18
    use what you know, 8, 12, 16
Like + infinitive, 8
Luján, Jorge (Argentinian poet), 12

M

Making plans, 13, 15
May and *might* (for possible future), 15
Money, 10, 11, VH
Months of the year, GS

N

Nouns
    count and non-count, 11
    plural, 2, 4
    possessive, 3
    singular, 2–4
Numbers, GS, 2, 3

O

Objects
    classroom, GS, 3
    household, 7
    of verbs, 16

P

Paragraphs, indenting, 2–3
Parties, 5, 7–9, 18
Parts of the body, 13, 15, 18
Past continuous tense, 14
Past tense
    of *be*, 6
    of *do*, 9, 10
    of irregular verbs, 9
    of regular verbs, 9
    with *used to*, 18
Personal information, 5
Prepositions of location, 4
Present continuous tense, 7–8
Present tense
    of *be*, 1, 5
    of *have*, 2
    of regular verbs, 5
    vs. present continuous, 8
Pronouns
    demonstrative, 3
    object, 7
    possessive, 14
    subject, 1, 7

Q

Questions with
    how, 10
    how much, 10
    how often, 16
    what, 5–8, 10, 13–15
    when, 10
    where, 4, 10
    who, 10
    whose, 14
    why, 10

R

Regular verbs, 5, 9
Restaurant, ordering food in a, 11
Rooms
    at home, 7, VH
    at school, 4, VH

S

Safety, 13–14
School
    exams, 15–18
    schedules, 2, 16
    subjects, 2, 4, 14–16, VH
Seasons, VH
Setting goals, 15
Shapes, VH
Shopping
    in a CD store, 12
    in a department store, 10
    in a supermarket, 11
Should (for giving advice), 17
Silent *e*, 7–8, 10–12
So, 11
Some and *any*, 11
Statements (affirmative and negative)
    in future tense with *going to*, 13
    in future tense with *will*, 15
    in past continuous tense, 14
    in past tense, 9
    in present continuous tense, 7
    with *be*, past tense, 6
    with *be*, present tense, 1
    with *can*, 5
    with *have*, present tense, 2
    with *like/have/want* + infinitive, 8
    with *may* and *might*, 15
    with regular verbs, present tense, 5
    with *should*, 17
    with *some* and *any*, 11
    with *there is* and *there are*, 4
    with *used to*, 18
Studying, 15–16

T

Telephone calls, 7–8, 13
There is and *there are*, 4
Time, GS 6
Too and *not enough*, 18

U

Units of measurement, VH

V

Vowel sounds
    diphthong: /oi/, 16
    diphthong: /ou/, 17
    long: /ā/, 7–8
    long: /ē/, 9
    long: /ī/, 7, 10
    long: /ō/, 7, 11
    long: /yōo/, 7, 12
    r-controlled: /ûr/, 18
    short: /a/, /i/, /o/, 2
    short: /e/, /u/, 3
    variant: /ô/, 15
    variant: /ōo/, 13
    variant: /ŏo/, 14
Vowels, 1, 3

W

Want + infinitive, 8
Weather and climate, 14, VH
Writing
    a dialogue, 7, 13
    a journal, 6
    a letter, 9, 17
    a paragraph, 1–4, 8, 11, 14–16
    a script, 10
    a story, 18
    words for a song, 12

Y

Yes/No questions
    in future tense with *going to*, 13
    in future tense with *will*, 15
    in past continuous tense, 14
    in past tense, 9
    in present continuous tense, 7
    with *be*, past tense, 6
    with *be*, present tense, 1
    with *can*, 5
    with *have*, present tense, 2
    with *like/have/want* + infinitive, 8
    with regular verbs, present tense, 5
    with *should*, 17
    with *used to*, 18

Credits

Text Credit

Jorge Luján. "A Fleeting Dozen," by Jorge Luján. "In the Darkness," by Jorge Luján. Printed by permission.

Illustration Credits

Mike DiGiorgio 208-209 (background), 219; **John Hovell** 12 top, 127, 161, 181, 200, 213, 215, 216, 225 top, 229 top; **Christopher Pavely** 14-15, 18, 19, 24, 25, 28, 29, 34, 35, 38, 39, 44, 45, 50, 51, 56, 57, 60, 61, 66, 67, 70, 71, 76, 82, 83, 88, 89, 92, 93, 98, 99, 102, 103, 108, 109, 114, 115, 120, 121, 124, 125, 130, 131, 134, 135, 140, 141, 146, 147, 152, 153, 156, 157, 162, 163, 166, 167, 172, 173, 178, 179, 184, 185, 188, 189, 194, 195, 198, 199, 204, 205; **William Waitzman** 4-12 bottom, 13, 20, 32, 40-43, 52, 54, 55, 64, 72, 74, 84-86, 96, 106, 118, 119, 126, 128, 136-139, 150, 151, 159, 160, 170, 182, 190, 192, 201, 202, 222-225 bottom, 226-229 bottom, 230-233, 236, 250, 257, 258.

Photo Credits

Cover, Getty Images; v bottom Rob Lewine/CORBIS; 2 (inset) Charles Gupton/StockBoston; iv bottom, 2-3 Getty Images; 3 (inset) Benelux Press/Index Stock Imagery; (images left to right) 13a Steve Sands/New York Newswire/CORBIS; 13b Reuters NewMedia/CORBIS; 13c Frank Trapper/CORBIS; 13d Reuters NewMedia/CORBIS; 16 (inset top) Spencer Grant/PhotoEdit; 16 (inset bottom) Jeff Greenberg/PhotoEdit; 16-17 Will & Deni McIntyre/Photo Researchers; iv top, v top, ix, 21, 23 David Young-Wolff/PhotoEdit; 33 Ronnie Kaufman/CORBIS; 48 (inset) Jonathan Nourok/PhotoEdit; 48-49 Michael Newman/PhotoEdit; 49 (inset) Network Productions/Index Stock Imagery; 53 Bohden Hrynewych/Stock Boston/Picture Quest; 62 Gary Conner/PhotoEdit; 73 Michael Newman/PhotoEdit; 80 (inset) Getty Images; 80-81 Michelle D. Bridwell/PhotoEdit; 81 (inset) CORBIS; 87 Tony Freeman/PhotoEdit; 94 Chuck Savage/CORBIS; 97 Michael Newman/PhotoEdit; 105, 144 (inset top) Getty Images; 112 (inset), 116, 129, 144-145, 144 (inset bottom), 171 David Young-Wolff/PhotoEdit; 112-113 Gabe Palmer/CORBIS; 149 Randy Wells/CORBIS; 169 Food Pix/Getty Images; 176 (left inset) Getty Images; 176 (right inset) Rob Lewine/CORBIS; 176-177 Paul A. Souders/CORBIS; 180 Richard Hutchings/PhotoEdit; 183 Michael Newman/PhotoEdit; 191 Bob Daemmrich/PhotoEdit; 193 Getty Images; 203 Raoul Minsart/CORBIS; 208 (inset), 220 right AP/Wide World Photos; 209 (inset), 217 Jorge Luján; 208-209, 210 Photowood/CORBIS; 211 (all) DK Images; 212 top Roger Ressmeyer/CORBIS; 212 bottom NASA/DK Images; 218 DK Images; 220 left Bettmann/CORBIS; 221 Flip Schulke/Black Star; (images left to right) 222a Michael Newman/PhotoEdit; 222b Ted Horowitz/CORBIS; 222c David Young-Wolff/PhotoEdit; 222d Frank Siteman/Omni-Photo Communications; 222e David Young-Wolff/PhotoEdit; 222f CORBIS; 222g Getty Images; 222h Fotopic/Omni-Photo Communications; 222i David Young-Wolff/PhotoEdit; 222j Michael Newman/PhotoEdit; 222k Lawrence Migdale/Pix; 222L Getty Images; (images left to right) 226a, 226b DK Images; 226c Getty Images; 226d DK Images; 226e Cary Wolinsky/Aurora & Quanta Productions; 226f DK Images; 226g Getty Images; 226h, 226i, 226j, 226k DK Images; 226L Becky Luigart-Stayner/CORBIS; (images left to right) 233a, 233b, 233c Getty Images; 233d Simon Harris/Robert Harding World Imagery; 233e David Young-Wolff/PhotoEdit; 233f J.P. Nacivet/Getty Images; 233g Rick Gomez/CORBIS; 233h David Stoecklein/CORBIS; 233i Mark L. Stephenson/CORBIS; 233j, 233k Getty Images; 233L Jose Luis Pelaez/CORBIS; 255 top right CORBIS; 255 bottom left Danny Lehman/CORBIS; 255 bottom right Charles & Josette Lenars/CORBIS.